"I'm an avid follower of Jonathan's thoughts and body of work. Jonathan's book *Igniting the Phoenix: A New Vision for IT* and interviews captured exactly what is now transpiring in terms of business transformation. I have quoted Jonathan on many, many occasions; his insights into understanding emerging key business issues both from the IT perspective and the line-of-business have been truly visionary."

Rod Smith, VP Internet Emerging Technology, IBM

"Jon is a wonderfully talented, exceptionally creative, and forward-thinking luminary that would be an asset to any technology team looking to add significant value to their organization and leap-frog their thinking. Jon has proven time and again that he can think things through, not only at a practical level, but also at a level of fore-thought that few venture."

Ron Schmelzer, Principal Analyst, Cognilytica

"Jonathan has a deep understanding of leading edge application development environments and a very practical sense of how best to apply technology for business gain. He is a visionary who has survived the technology wars with valuable experience and insight."

David Shimberg, Strategic Advisor, iDeliver Technologies LLC

Thriving at the Edge of Chaos

Books by Jonathan Sapir

Mastering Untamed Business Processes
How to Build Smart Process Applications on the Salesforce Platform (2015)

Smart Process App
The Next Breakout Business Advantage (with Peter Fingar and Craig le Clair) *(2013)*

The Executives Guide to Force.com
Enabling Shadow IT and Citizen Developers in the Age of Cloud Computing (2012)

Unleash the Power of Force.com
How to Thrive in the New Digital Economy (2011)

Power in the Cloud
Using Cloud Computing to Build Information Systems at the Edge of Chaos (2009)

Igniting the Phoenix
A New Vision for IT (2003)

Thriving at the Edge of Chaos
Managing Projects as Complex Adaptive Systems

Jonathan Sapir

Routledge
Taylor & Francis Group
A PRODUCTIVITY PRESS BOOK

First edition published in 2020
by Routledge/Productivity Press
52 Vanderbilt Avenue, 11th Floor, New York, NY 10017
2 Park Square, Milton Park, Abingdon, Oxon, OX14 4RN, UK

© 2020 by Jonathan Sapir

Routledge/Productivity Press is an imprint of Taylor & Francis Group, an Informa business

No claim to original U.S. Government works

Printed on acid-free paper

International Standard Book Number-13: 978-0-367-40464-2 (Paperback)
International Standard Book Number-13: 978-0-429-35658-2 (eBook)
International Standard Book Number-13: 978-0-367-40540-3 (Hardback)

Library of Congress Cataloging-in-Publication Data
Names: Sapir, Jonathan, author.
Title: Thriving at the edge of chaos : managing projects as complex adaptive systems / Jonathan Sapir.
Description: Boca Raton : Taylor & Francis, 2020. | Includes bibliographical references and index.
Identifiers: LCCN 2019036884 (print) | LCCN 2019036885 (ebook) | ISBN 9780367404642 (paperback) | ISBN 9780367405403 (hardback) | ISBN 9780429356582 (ebook)
Subjects: LCSH: Organizational change. | Project management. | Success in business.
Classification: LCC HD58.8 .S267 2020 (print) | LCC HD58.8 (ebook) | DDC 658.4/04–dc23
LC record available at https://lccn.loc.gov/2019036884
LC ebook record available at https://lccn.loc.gov/2019036885

Visit the Taylor & Francis Web site at www.taylorandfrancis.com

The Edge of Chaos

The term itself suggests something has gone wrong, but operating at the edge of chaos is actually healthy; scientists have shown that all large and complex systems tend to adapt this way. Whether in nature, society, economics, – or project management – systems must find the right balance between order and flexibility. This is because their survival and success depend on being able to constantly sense and adapt to changes in the environment they operate within.

In a business context, operating at the edge of chaos opens up avenues for disruptive innovation, cultural overhaul, and process evolution, all of which help organizations adapt to changing market environments.

BBVA, Order from Chaos: How to Apply Complexity Theory at Work

Contents

Preface

> If I had asked people what they wanted, they would have said
> faster horses.
>
> *Henry Ford*

This book describes how applying Complexity Science can dramatically help improve the practice of project management.

The book originated from an idea based on work which my consulting company, SilverTree Systems, did about six years ago for three companies in very different industries: a global Contract Research Organization (CRO) that runs clinical trials across the world for pharmaceutical companies; a Fortune 100 fast-food franchise company that installs new equipment periodically across thousands of stores worldwide; and a digital marketing company that runs multi-media projects for global organizations. All three organizations faced similar problems:

- **Planning:** It was impossible to map out the complexity of the work to be done in a Gantt chart, resulting in missing tasks and dependencies.
- **Scheduling:** Schedules changed continuously, resulting in an enormous waste of project management time.
- **Execution:** There was no way to get an early warning that a project was potentially in trouble so that action could be taken before it became a problem, resulting in late project delivery.
- **Status:** Status reporting by percent complete was essentially meaningless, as "90 percent complete" frequently persisted for extended periods of time.
- **Resources:** Key resources were often unavailable when needed, resulting in continuously changing priorities and fights over resource assignments.

Along with the ever-growing need to complete more projects faster with fewer resources these problems were seriously impacting their businesses. It was clear that simply tweaking the way projects were being managed would never produce the kind of leap in production that they were looking for. It required a completely new way of thinking about the problem.

So we set out to build a solution.

It was obvious that unless we found a completely new approach we would end up with another me-too project management system based on the same ideas that haven't advanced significantly in decades and clearly weren't up to the task faced by these companies.

I started by looking for new ideas in other industries. The obvious examples of radical change were new companies like Uber and AirBnB. What did they do that was so successful in disrupting their industries?

This led me to the relatively new world of Complexity Science.

New business models like Uber show us that the most efficient operations behave like Complex Adaptive Systems (CAS) where self-managing participants, following a set of simple rules, organize themselves to solve incredibly complex problems. Instead of trying to function like a "well-oiled machine" where things "work like clockwork", Uber functions more like a living organism, a system constantly changing and adapting. It fully embraces characteristics of a CAS.

A CAS is a complex system that has the capacity to adapt. It is a collection of individual agents with the freedom to act in ways that are not always totally predictable, and whose actions are interconnected so that one agent's actions change the context of other agents. It is adaptive because its activities adjust or react to the events of the environment in a way that facilitates or allows the system to achieve its purpose.

Complexity Science proposes new ways to look at age-old problems with a fresh perspective. It is based on an appreciation of the unpredictable and interconnected relationships that occur within a complex system – like a project management environment. It completely changes the way managers think about the problems they face.

In fact, what we usually identify as "problems" to be controlled and avoided (e.g. uncertainty, variability, conflicts) are just evidence of a complex nature. You cannot predict or absolutely control the future, so pretending that you can may feel more comfortable but is ultimately far more dangerous than accepting a degree of unpredictability and being prepared for the unexpected.[1]

The question then became: How can CAS thinking be applied to the field of project management?

The objective of this book is to explain how adopting a CAS-based paradigm can lead to innovative work management solutions that are much better suited to the volatile, uncertain, and rapidly changing world in which we operate our organizations. The result is a comprehensive approach that will power the next generation of work management solutions and give companies a competitive edge.

The book has two objectives:

1. Make these ideas accessible to anyone – executives, business managers, project managers, business analysts – without having to read through reams of books and articles.
2. Spark questions, critiques, and suggestions to help refine this approach to work management.

I have no doubt that reading this book will radically change how you think about managing projects. I hope you enjoy it and find it illuminating.

I look forward to hearing from you. Please email me at jon@work-relay.com. And remember to keep an open mind!

Jonathan Sapir

Note

1. Complexity Theory, Mosaic Projects.

Acknowledgments

My interest in Complex Adaptive Systems (CAS) has taken me on a fascinating journey, from Michal Crichton's books *The Lost World* and *Jurassic Park* to the videos provided by the *Systems Academy*. The bibliography covers just a fraction of what I read over the years, and while my research didn't turn me into an expert on CAS, it provided enough understanding to apply the ideas of CAS to project management.

There are a number of people who have contributed to the book, including Mark Woeppel (Pinnacle Strategies), Wolfram Müller (Speed4projects), Michael Clingan (The Claymore Group), Eli Schragenheim (Elyakim Management Systems), Scott Perry (Tegna), and Scott Wilson (Calisto Media).

I would like to acknowledge my enormously talented team at Work-Relay for turning the theory into reality.

My enormous thanks to Kristine Mednansky for seeing value in the book and getting it published, and to everyone in the Taylor & Francis Group for helping get the book into a publishable state.

I would especially like to acknowledge Iris Mae for always keeping me amused, Daniel Levi for his persistence in getting me to finish the book, and my wife and family for their love and support.

About the Author

Jonathan Sapir has over 30 years' experience helping clients leverage information technology to build their businesses. Jonathan is the founder and CEO of SilverTree Systems, Inc., a mid-sized global software development company. SilverTree clients include Adobe, Docusign, CNA, LifeFitness, and Taco Bell. Jonathan started his career as a systems engineer for IBM South Africa where he was responsible for implementing emerging technologies.

Jonathan is also the founder and CEO of Work-Relay, an innovative Enterprise Work Management System built on the Salesforce platform. Work-Relay has been implemented across a wide range of industries, from start-ups to Fortune 100 companies.

Overview

I think the next century will be the century of complexity.

Stephen Hawking, January 2000

Complexity in business is a fast-growing problem. Inflexibility, and the inability to quickly adapt to changing circumstances, are chronic inhibitors to the success of every organization. In this increasingly dynamic and unpredictable world, workers must respond to constant change and deal with an environment full of exceptions. These problems are becoming more critical as companies face tougher competition, expand globally, increase outsourcing, and need to cope with an increasingly chaotic world.

Companies are operating in vastly more complex conditions than existed just a decade ago, with the emergence of new technologies, greater customer variety, global operations, and shifting regulations. Many are discovering that the frameworks and strategies they commonly turn to are no longer effective. Companies need fresh insights.

The organization pays for this complexity in delayed time-to-market, slow customer response, and decreased productivity.

For many organizations, the way in which projects are managed is a fundamental factor in how well they can prosper in today's marketplace. By improving efficiency, driving productivity, and reducing costs, organizations can increase throughput, improve service, and bring new products to market faster.

Unfortunately, the current solutions available to companies for managing projects in this environment have limited capacity to meet these challenges effectively and are unlikely to have the kind of impact they need. Tweaking the current project environment may provide some minimal gains, but to have a real impact requires a change in mindset.

The Impact of Paradigms

Every kind of management is based on an accepted worldview, or paradigm. We just operate under that paradigm and try to optimize it by, for example, sending more people to training, or hiring better project managers. These things may give you a small boost in production, but they are not going to be game changers for your organization.

At some point, we cannot get better within the paradigm anymore. That's why, for example, all project management systems look so much the same.

This is when we are given a choice: we can either accept that we have reached the end of the line and stay within that paradigm. Or we can shift the paradigm.

Shifting the Paradigm

There's nothing physical or expensive about paradigm change. In a single individual, it can happen in a millisecond. All it takes is a click in the mind, a new way of seeing. Of course, individuals and societies do resist challenges to their paradigm harder than they resist any other kind of change.[1]

But if you can intervene at the level of paradigm you can totally transform the system. This is basically the story of Uber and AirBnB. The concept of getting a ride in some stranger's car or sleeping at some stranger's apartment seemed ludicrous at first. But once people changed their thinking from "that seems unsafe" to "why not?" the paradigm shift was complete.

Uber is a perfect example of a company that understood the impact of shifting paradigms. Uber wasn't interested in a 10 to 15 percent improvement in the functioning of its industry – Uber wanted to disrupt the industry. They weren't going to get this by tinkering with the current paradigm. For example, Uber didn't try to come up with a better algorithm for scheduling taxi drivers. It just eliminated scheduling (and taxi drivers!) altogether. This is the kind of paradigm shift we need if we are to radically increase process and project production.

New business models like Uber show us that the most efficient operations behave like Complex Adaptive Systems (CAS) where self-managing participants, following a set of simple rules, organize themselves to solve incredibly complex problems. Instead of trying to function like a "well-oiled machine" where things "work like clockwork", Uber functions more like a living organism that is alive and constantly changing. It fully embraces characteristics of a CAS.

Applying a Complexity Mindset

CAS thinking is a way of challenging taken-for-granted assumptions about how people, organizations, and systems interact. Viewing an organization as a Complex Adaptive System drives a new philosophy of project management.

So, to get the quantum leap improvement in work and project production that we are looking for, we need to question the underlying assumptions that support the paradigm and replace them with something that is more likely to give us the results we are looking for. This requires killing the sacred cows upon which traditional project management is based, and indeed, by establishing a different mindset or worldview – by shifting paradigms.

For example, instead of constantly scheduling and re-scheduling task deadlines, what if we do away with task deadlines altogether? What if we eliminate the need to match resources with constantly changing schedules and priorities? What if we dispensed with Gantt charts, a 100-plus-year-old invention designed for a different time and a different purpose, as a way to plan and manage projects? What if we recognize that percent complete is a subjective, backward-looking metric that isn't much better than a set of random numbers?

Only by asking questions like these will we be able to shift the paradigm that governs how we currently manage projects in the enterprise and replace it with a radically different solution that is much better suited to the needs of the twenty-first-century organization.

The Impact of Complexity Thinking

Adopting a different frame of reference changes one's perspective so that what was remote and unnatural becomes sensible and natural. If the world you work in is complex, then acting congruently with that complexity can be simpler than trying to control it like a machine that doesn't exist.

What we usually identify as "problems" to be controlled and avoided (uncertainty, variability, conflicts) are just evidence of a complex nature. You cannot predict or absolutely control the future, so pretending you can feel more comfortable is ultimately far more dangerous than accepting a degree of unpredictability and being prepared for the unexpected.

Conclusion

To adopt complexity thinking, you first need to understand the basics of Complexity Science. If you don't understand how complexity works, you cannot understand how your management approach impacts the complexity of your work environment.

We can then apply this knowledge to the management of projects.

This book exposes the assumptions underlying the accepted paradigm of project management, describes the common practices that are based on those assumptions, analyzes why these practices are unhelpful and even harmful, and proposes alternative, sometimes seemingly counter-intuitive approaches to work management.

By the end of the book, you will have a completely new perspective on the way projects can be managed in your organization, and how you can quickly start reaping the benefits provided by a project management methodology and supporting toolset that is more in tune with the demands of the twenty-first century, and turns complexity into a competitive advantage.

Note

1. *Systems Practice: How to Act: In Situations of Uncertainty and Complexity in a Climate Change World*, Ray Ison, Springer.

Introduction

Our Age of Anxiety is, in a great part, the result of trying to do today's job with yesterday's tools and yesterday's concepts.

Marshall McLuhan

The number of project management systems currently flooding the marketplace is nothing short of astounding. Sadly, they all tend to be variations of the same tired thinking that hasn't changed much in decades. Most of the solutions just prop up the status quo, doing more of the same, just trying harder rather than thinking of fresh underlying assumptions.

But what used to be accepted wisdom no longer applies in an accelerated business world that has grown significantly more complex.

And yet, for many organizations, the need to elevate project performance is critical for competitive strategy. In project-based businesses, doing more projects faster is the way to increase revenues, profit margins, and rate of return on investments. For new product development organizations, shrinking life cycles require more projects to be done quicker with the same assets. In companies doing things like equipment installation and maintenance, cutting turnaround time and lowering manpower resources allows organizations to complete more projects on time at reduced costs.[1] And there are also many companies that are not primarily project-based that run repetitive projects. For example, a food franchise company like Taco Bell periodically needs to install new equipment in all its thousands of stores. All of these organizations are heavily dependent on managing projects as efficiently and effectively as possible.

And, now that rapid technological advancements are driving our world to higher and higher magnitudes of interconnectivity, organizations are encountering complex systems with even greater frequency and consequence. So it is more important than ever for organizations to understand complexity and consider ways in which Complexity Science can help.

What is a Project?

A good place to start is to clarify what a project actually is.

(Note: This book applies primarily to repetitive, as opposed to one-off, never-to-be-done-again projects. It does not apply to software development projects that use agile methodology.)

The Project Management Institute (PMI) defines a project as a temporary endeavor undertaken to create a unique product, service, or result. So, if the endeavor is a one-time occurrence, never to be repeated, it is, according to this definition, a project. Examples include things like a project to move the headquarters of the company to a new location. It's one-and-done.

But most companies have "projects" that are not temporary, one-off affairs. Rather, they repeat, like running clinical drug trials, installing equipment for customers, or running marketing campaigns.

These types of projects are really not projects in the PMI sense at all – they are processes that are managed as projects.

This is important because the tools used to manage processes and projects are quite different in their approach. For example, because projects are assumed to run only once, you must plan them every time, and the effort must pay off from the outcome of the one time you execute the project. Repetitive projects, on the other hand, are obviously repeatable. The fact that the activities are repeated means that you can effectively amortize the planning effort over many repetitions.

Repetitive projects are also typically much more complex to manage than one-off projects, in that there are many instances of the project running concurrently, and these projects usually share the same resources.

The stakes are high for many repetitive projects. They have an important impact on how the organization does business. They create winners and losers. Having the right tools to address these needs is often a mission-critical factor. If your organization runs process-driven projects, and you are managing them as projects, you are severely limiting your organizations capabilities.

The Assumptions of Traditional Project Management

Like any type of management, project management is based on a common set of assumptions.

Ensuring tasks complete on time is the best way to ensure that the project completes on time.
The idea that if every task is on time the project will be on time is burdened with unintended consequences: task estimates will be inflated to consider the variability of task execution; task dates ensure that no task will ever be early, but late tasks will impact the schedule, and multi-tasking is sure to be rampant.

Adding padding to task estimates helps ensure that they will be completed on time.
Inflated estimates encourage bad behavior, like Student Syndrome (waiting until the last minute for the task to be started, knowing the task has extra time built into it) and Parkinson's Law (filling the time allotted regardless of need).

The future is essentially controllable.
It is possible to "predict" failure and mitigate it through big upfront planning. Management has control over the worker's actions, and consequently the project outcome can be achieved through developing accurate schedules and cost plans with adequate levels of detail and proper risk assessments incorporated into the plans; and then diligently managing in accordance with those plans. The natural extension of these ideas is that if adequate control cannot be achieved at the current level of decomposition, adding more detail will bring "better control" and that human destiny is controllable. This incorrectly assumes that all is knowable beforehand.

It's possible to manage or eliminate "all risk".
If adequate effort is applied to risk management, all risks can be transferred, mitigated or identified for acceptance, and appropriate contingencies and risk response plans can be calculated for all of the accepted risks.

Percent complete is the best way to track task and project status.
Percent complete is a backward-looking, subjective, essentially meaningless measure of project and task status that leads to a prolonged "90 percent completed" syndrome.

Projects should be started as early as possible to help ensure they are completed on time.
Starting projects as soon as possible slows everything down if the system doesn't have the capacity to handle them.

Tasks should be started as early as possible to help ensure they are completed on time.
Starting tasks as soon as possible leads to dilution of focus on the part of the project manager and team if the task does not have all the prerequisites in place. It can also lead to unnecessary multi-tasking, rework, and poor decision making.

100 percent resource utilization is an appropriate goal for the organization.
Managers worry about keeping individuals "busy" in their project planning. Nothing else matters as long as they are optimizing at a functional level. But keeping people busy is not the objective of the project, and trying to achieve 100 percent resource utilization for all resources is worse than a waste of time – it robs managers of precious management and with no buffer, guarantees that 100 percent of your projects will be late.

Multi-tasking is a good way to make progress on multiple projects.
Multi-tasking to get multiple projects completed as quickly as possible is highly inefficient when someone is waiting for the output of your task before they can start theirs.

If we optimize each area involved in the project, we can increase project throughput.
Trying to optimize anything other than the constraint for improving overall project throughput diffuses the resources and energy available for improvement.

Gantt charts are the best way to plan and manage a project.
The core of every project management system is a Gantt chart. Gantt charts are used for managing all aspects of project management: planning, scheduling, execution, and monitoring.

Unfortunately, Gantt charts are littered with minefields, many of which most project managers are barely aware of:

Ill-deserved credibility
The visual quality of color charts means that they gain an implicit credibility. This can result in managers being unwilling to challenge the charts and so they gain a momentum all of their own. They encourage the project manager to over-control the project rather than to devolve responsibility for the time plan to team members.

continued on page 6

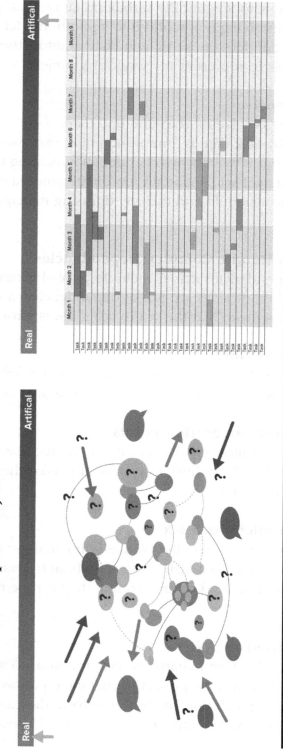

Figure I.1 On the left is how project managers really experience a project, while on the right is a manipulated and distorted version of events. The project has been manipulated to look harmonious, ordered, and in control.

The Gantt chart smooths out the turbulent, emotional, punctuated, messy, and unforgiving real world into smooth, modernist, calming, and confident lines. A Gantt chart is altogether the wrong piece of artwork to represent the work of a project.

It's Work Intensive

Every task must be given a start and end date.

Scheduling by task date is a mind-numbing exercise in futility given that the dates will always change, guaranteeing that the project manager will spend an inordinate amount of time maintaining the schedule and thereby diffusing management attention.

It's Unable to Handle Complex Dependencies

Visualizing dependencies across multiple pages becomes impossible. When projects are full of dependencies, a missed dependency can mean that the entire schedule is wrong.

It Doesn't Show Holes

If there are gaps between tasks because the dependencies weren't specified, you are not going to know this from the Gantt chart.

It Doesn't Show Integration Points

For example, if a milestone has multiple tasks required for its completion, and each of those tasks has sub-tasks, the Gantt chart cannot depict this well.

It's a Poor Predictor of Risk

The Gantt chart shows only the planned and actual start and completion dates for each task. It does nothing to warn of potential problems ahead of time so that they can be dealt with before it's too late.

It's Task-Focused

A major flaw is that Gantt charts are task-focused, so when a new task is discovered the project is guaranteed to be late. Also, tasks will take as much time as they are given: they are rarely completed early, and any time a task is late it will delay the project.

It Doesn't Reveal Conditional Paths

If a project can go down different paths (with an alternate set of tasks) based on conditions that become apparent as the project progresses, there is no way to depict this on a Gantt chart.

Typical Problems with Traditional Project Management

These assumptions may have worked in a world that moved slower, but they are wildly lacking for today's business environment.

- **Planning:** It was impossible to map out the complexity of the work to be done on a Gantt chart, resulting in missing tasks and dependencies.
- **Scheduling:** Schedules changed continuously, resulting in an enormous waste of project management time.
- **Execution:** There was no way to get an early warning that a project was potentially in trouble so that action could be taken before it became a problem, resulting in late project delivery.
- **Resources:** Key resources were often unavailable when needed, resulting in continuously changing priorities and fights over resource assignments.

As a result, they lead to a plethora of common project management problems, including the following:

- Task durations padded with contingency still miss their dates.
- There are too many schedule changes.
- There are fights about priorities between projects.
- Resources are not available to work when needed.
- Shifting priorities cause widespread multi-tasking.
- More work is pushed into the system than the system can successfully handle.
- There are too many status meetings that are too frequent and too long.
- Managers over-react to noise and under-react to real risks.
- Status reporting is painful.
- Status reporting by percent complete was essentially meaningless, as "90 percent complete" frequently persisted for extended periods of time.

■ There are tasks that are critical bottlenecks and hurt the entire operation due to their limited capacity.

■ There is a lot of waiting for all feeding legs of the project to come together at integration points.

■ There is a lot of waiting for decisions or for issues to be resolved, because managers have too much on their plates.

■ Not all the necessary information is transitioned among workers upon completion of steps.

■ Team members forget to do necessary steps, or do them out of sequence.

■ Project managers fail to take advantage of early task completions.

■ Team members are measured on metrics that encourage bad behavior.

■ Solving these types of problems can only be done by challenging the underlying assumptions on which project management systems are built. Without doing this, it is impossible for organizations to make a quantum leap forward in project performance.

Typical Responses to Project Management Challenges

Instead of questioning the underlying assumptions, the response to these problems usually comes down to one or more of the following.

Moving the Finishing Line

The level of lateness is sometimes hard to identify clearly, because when it is clear that dates will be missed, they often change. **We're no longer considered late if the date is moved out**. There are many justifications for this "moving finish line" syndrome: changes to scope, acts of God, vendor problems, and so on. Given the emphasis on deadlines, it isn't surprising that people would want to point fingers away from themselves when deadlines are in jeopardy.

Deadline systems tend to be homeostatic relative to their deadline dates. They seek equilibrium around those dates. If a project or task is late, people work hard to get it back on track, sometimes working weekends and evenings to make it happen. If a project or task is early, people relax, maybe shuffling resources to something more urgent. There are pressures that move things earlier and later. Most project organizations are self-correcting as they try to hit their dates. Speed – above whatever is needed to hit deadlines – is agonizingly difficult.[2]

Spend More Time on Planning

If things didn't work out as well as we'd like, maybe we just didn't plan well enough at the start of the project. Maybe the requirements gathering was insufficient, or our estimates weren't good enough. To rectify this, maybe we should spend more time planning – involve more people in the planning process, spend more time reviewing the plans, find the parts that need to be reworked or clarified.

Of course, poor planning is a recipe for poor outcomes, but planning is one of those things that are subject to the law of diminishing returns. Beyond a certain level, more time and money in planning yields fewer and fewer benefits. There's a limit to predicting the future. Contrast the tactic that "more planning is the solution" with the way construction engineers use a tactic to protect their high-rise buildings that takes a different road. Rather than trying to improve earthquake predictability, their focus is on protecting the building from the effects of the earthquake. They accept that predictability is imperfect. But they refuse to accept that this uncertainty cannot be mitigated in a different manner. Their focus instead is to employ tactics that mitigate the effect of uncertainty, rather than to reduce the uncertainty itself. The focus of improving project planning is like focusing on better earthquake prediction – which will always still fall short of complete 100 percent predictability.

Hire "Great Individuals" Capable of Absorbing the Complexity of Unknowns

Many organizations assume that project problems are due to lack of skill and knowledge among project managers and teams. So the most common approach to the problem is training, education, and employing very experienced project managers.

"Great fire-fighters" working on projects are the dream of many organizations. If we just had enough of the right people on the team, and enough "A players" who could "pull this off", then we could keep projects on track. If we've got people capable of juggling all the complexity, and readjusting everything whenever unexpected events occur, then maybe we'll get more certain outcomes.

There's no question that more capable people are better than less capable people at patching and closing the gaps and disturbances in a project. But what do you think would be the outcome if the project system itself rather than the people were better able to absorb that uncertainty and complexity the way a building's seismic dampeners do in an earthquake?

Minimize the Damage and Make the Best Trade-offs

The fourth tactic in traditional project management is of course to simply try to minimize the damage. Unexpected events occur, so let's minimize the losses. This usually means negotiating scope, cost, schedule, or quality compromises to the project and trying to find the least damaging trade-offs.

The Need for a New Response

> It is not necessary to change. Survival is not mandatory.
>
> *W. Edwards Deming*

Needless to say, these responses are not helpful in resolving the underlying causes of project management dysfunction.

The world is becoming more and more complex, interconnected, and more difficult for even excellent people to mitigate against. The only real choice you have is to evolve your methodologies and systems to better cope with this complexity.

Without questioning the underlying assumptions upon which today's project management is based, the improvements that can be made are limited at best. As we will see, questioning these assumptions and replacing them with a more realistic understanding of how things really work will allow us to take a quantum leap forward in how we manage our projects.

How the Book is Organized

If you don't understand how complexity works, you cannot understand how your management approach impacts the complexity in your work environment.

So the first part of the book provides a tour through the contributions of Complexity Science, and then analyzes each aspect of project management – planning, scheduling, execution, monitoring, resourcing, and optimization – and shows how you can practically apply Complexity Science to more effectively manage projects in your organization.

Part I Understanding Complexity

How does Complexity Science help us rethink the traditional ways in which we manage work so that we can better respond to the challenges of work management in the twenty-first century?

The first thing is to understand what a paradigm is, why it's important, and why it is the key to radical change. Then we'll take a journey through scientific thinking, from Newton's clockwork universe and Frederick Taylor's Scientific Management to the new world of Systems Thinking, Complexity Science and Complex Adaptive Systems (CAS).

The objective is to show how thinking about how the world works has progressed, and to see how project management methodology has been left behind.

The ultimate goal is to learn how to apply this new way of thinking to the problems faced in project management, and get to a point where a practical implementation can take place.

Part II Project Management as a Complex Adaptive System

Part 2 applies the lessons of Complexity Science to the key areas of project management.

Platform

How do you design a system capable of handling any type of work?

Design

How can an organization be more flexible and adaptive in a dynamic, volatile business environment?

Estimate

How can you manage the inevitable variation in task estimates so that (1) time is not wasted, and (2) that don't cause a project to be late?

Schedule

How can you eliminate the drain of scheduling and re-scheduling on the project manager's time?

Execute

How do you ensure that work can navigate through layers of complexity so that it can move smoothly across the organization as quickly as possible?

Resource

How can you manage resources effectively when change is constant without spending an inordinate amount of time?

Monitor

How can you objectively measure how a project is progressing and get an early warning when things need management attention?

Optimize

How can you maximize your resources to increase throughput?

Implement

How can you implement these ideas in your organization in an effective and non-disruptive manner?

Notes

1. This book applies primarily to repetitive, as opposed to one-off, never-to-be-done-again projects. It does not apply to software development projects that use agile methodology.
2. *The tyranny of deadline solutions*, Rob Newbold, CEO, Prochain Solutions, Inc.

UNDERSTANDING COMPLEXITY

The goal is to thrive at the edge of chaos and surf the emerging wave of reality – and doing it without getting swept away in the tide.

The surfer is constantly getting feedback by taking in information about their present state and constantly making minor corrections in many dimensions (heading, speed, balance, etc.). The weaving is the result of the surfer maintaining dynamic equilibrium while moving toward their goal. Using feedback to stay within the limits of tolerance of the many aspects of their system.

Instead of wasting a lot of time and energy predicting the exact "right" path up front, surfers instead hold their purpose in mind, stay present in the moment, and find the most natural path to their goal as they go.

Chapter 1

The Current Paradigm

The greatest challenge facing project management in the 21st
Century is managing the shift from the "command and control"
paradigm based in the theories of "scientific management"
developed by Taylor and others in the early 20th Century to a
recognition of the inherent uncertainty and complexity involved in
managing every project, and in particular, projects focused on the
outputs of knowledge workers.

Patrick Weaver, Mosaic Project Services

What is a Paradigm?

A paradigm is a way of making sense of the world.

If you are going to manage anything, you have to have to have some
representation or model of how it works. A paradigm is the fundamental
conceptual framework or model we use for interpreting events and a way
of understanding the way the world works. Paradigms are the single most
determining factor for any and every outcome.

By definition, we believe the existing paradigm to be the right one and
therefore cannot imagine anything other than that at that point of time. If
you think that something functions like a machine, your solutions will be
based on fixing the machine. We just operate under that paradigm and try
to optimize it. We try to do the best we can to keep the mindset, thoughts,
and skills in place. At some point, however, we cannot get better within the
paradigm anymore. That's why all the project management systems out there
look the same.

This is when we are given a choice: we can either accept that we have reached the end of the line and stay within that paradigm. Or we can shift the paradigm.

A Paradigm Shift is a Powerful Change Accelerator

There's nothing physical or expensive or even slow about paradigm change. In a single individual, it can happen in a millisecond. All it takes is a click in the mind, a new way of seeing. Of course, individuals and societies do resist challenges to their paradigm harder than they resist any other kind of change.

But if you are able to intervene in systems at the level of paradigm, you hit a leverage point that totally transforms the systems. This is basically the story of Uber and AirBnB. The concept of getting a ride in some stranger's car or sleeping at some stranger's apartment seemed ludicrous at first. But once people changed their thinking from "that seems unsafe" to "why not?", the paradigm shift was complete.

The Current Paradigm

> [Reductionism] is the sin of modern life ... reducing things to their components and thereby, too often, missing the meaning and message of the forest in a minute examination of its trees.
>
> *Charles Handy*

Project management, like every other kind of management, is based on an accepted worldview, or paradigm.

The underlying paradigm of project management adopts a perspective which is primarily mechanistic, focusing on well-structured, centralized command and control. If what we are dealing with is a machine, then we just need to specify the parts well, and make sure that each part does what it is designed to do. If things get out of line, we need to get them "back on track".

Current project management tools and techniques are thus based on the assumption that with enough preplanning and control we are able to ensure that processes and projects will meet their objectives and complete on time. But this approach provides managers with unrealistic expectations of their ability to control outcomes.

So how did we get here?

Newtonianism

Since the time of the Renaissance, the predominant metaphor of science has been that of the machine. Scientists of the time described the universe as a grand clockwork. The planets spun around the Sun in predictable orbits and physical bodies moved in trajectories that could be described with the precision of mathematics. In this universe, the outcome of an action is predictable and repeatable, and outcomes (outputs) scale in proportion to inputs (i.e. more effort results in a larger or quicker output).

The goal of science was to reduce the world to its piece parts, to understand those parts, and then put them back together in new ways to make new things. And if we worked on the parts of these machines and made each part work better, then the whole would work better. This is called *reductionism*.

ISAAC NEWTON AND THE WORLD AS A "CLOCKWORK UNIVERSE"

- The world works like a machine – like a clock.
- "Machines" are simple and predictable.
- Every observed effect has an observable cause.
- Even very complicated phenomena can be understood through analysis. That is, the whole can be understood by taking it apart and studying the pieces.
- Sufficient analysis of past events can create the capacity to predict future events.
- The outcome of an action is predictable and repeatable.
- Outcomes (outputs) scale in proportion to inputs (i.e. more effort results in larger or quicker output).
- Change can be focused on specific areas, holding all other things constant.

In this way we can reduce complexity and risk, develop a plan, and then execute and rigorously control changes to the plan. If this is still complex you will need to take your analysis one step further and look at their components. If you continue this subdivision long enough you will end up with the smallest possible parts. The natural extension of these ideas is that if adequate control cannot be achieved at the current level of decomposition, adding more detail will bring "better control" and that human destiny is controllable.

These assumptions have proven extremely potent in developing our understanding of the physical world. Newton's "laws of nature" seemed so perfect and universal that they became the organizing principles of all post-feudal societies, including armies, churches, and economic institutions. They can be recognized by the continued use of Newtonian principles in the way we talk about, for example, the economy, which is said to "have momentum", is "well-oiled", or is "gaining steam".

This thinking pervades our view of leadership and management. Organization charts, job descriptions, corporate policies, detailed strategic and operational plans, and countless other artifacts of modern organizational life are deeply rooted in the machine metaphor. These are our attempts to specify, in increasing detail, the piece parts of organizational systems so that the overall clockwork of the organization can better produce the outcomes we desire.

Thus, Newtonianism accounts for the existence of inappropriate and monumental project management methodologies and explains why organizations develop elaborate systems, procedures, and policies in a futile attempt to get a grip on complex projects.

NEWTONIAN NEUROSIS[1]

Tim Lister, senior consultant and Fellow of the Cutter Consortium, calls the compulsive need to beat a complex project into a straight line *Newtonian neurosis*. Sufferers of Newtonian neurosis are called Flatliners. Flatliners relentlessly try to bludgeon every squiggly line in a project into submission through the excessive use of project management tools, rules, templates, policies, and procedures.

Sooner or later, Flatliners realize it's not working. They typically complain that the organization is not properly supporting them and does not believe in project management. They also admit their own shortcomings. If you were to peek into the head of a despondent project manager, the self-talk you hear might go something like this: "The world is not conforming to my plan. I must not be a good planner or project manager after all. I'd better take more project management courses and get more PDUs [professional development units]. I will do better and promise to use more templates and tools."

Newtonian neurosis leads to the futile practice of attempting to change the world to fit your plan, which is fiction in the first place. Why would anyone want to change reality to conform to fiction? Newtonian neurosis, that's why.

Scientific Management

Perhaps the most prominent single element in modern scientific management is the task idea. ... The work of every workman is fully planned out by the management at least one day in advance, and each man receives in most cases complete written instructions, describing in detail the task which he is to accomplish, as well as the means to be used in doing the work.

Frederick Winslow Taylor, The Principles of Scientific Management, 1911

The first attempt at management "science" was based on reductionism. In 1911, Frederick Winslow Taylor published his magnum opus, *The Principles of Scientific Management*, which laid out his ground rules for efficient industrial organization. Taylor's book is now a classic of managerial literature. His ideas have shaped companies across the industrial spectrum and defined the task of management for generations of managers.

In it, Taylor maintained that

it is only through enforced standardization of methods, enforced adoption of the best implements and working conditions, and enforced cooperation that this faster work can be assured. And the duty of enforcing the adoption of standards and enforcing this cooperation rests with the management alone.

Taylor's principles inaugurated a revolution in management and in the organization of work. In the decades following his book's publication, Taylor's ideas contributed to massive increases in productivity and the standard of living.

Taylor believed that you design what is to be produced and then look at each step of production, and break those steps into sub-steps. He watched workers carefully, and recorded exactly how much time and how much motion was necessary. Reduce the amount of motion and the work gets easier. Reduce the time and you can be more productive. It is an idea that fits perfectly with industrial age mechanization.

When Henry Ford designed his factory he took all these ideas into account, and the result was the first production automobile that could be mass produced at a price that a large part of the population could afford. What we need to remember is that Ford was in complete control of the factory line. Every aspect of building a car within that environment could be carefully controlled, and outside influences during production could be eliminated. In such a controlled environment, reductionism works fairly well.

But it fails to work in situations where organizations must respond to external pressures.

In fast-changing markets, the fragmentation of work, the separation of planning from execution, and the isolation of workers from each other create rigid organizations that cannot adapt quickly to change.

Project Management Manifestation

The key underpinnings of the theory of project management derive from the principles of "scientific management".

The core belief of the Project Management Institute (PMI) and many practitioners is that projects are logically deterministic initiatives which can be managed and controlled by a project manager with the appropriate skills. This assumes a perfect world: you create a good plan, track, and projects will get done.

This accounts for the existence of inappropriate and monumental project management methodologies and explains why organizations develop elaborate systems, procedures, and policies in a futile attempt to get a grip on complex projects.

The Current Paradigm Falls Apart

> All problems result from the mismatch between how the real-world systems work and how we think they work.
> – *Derek Cabrera and Laura Cabrera, Systems Thinking Made Simple*

Within a decade of the publication of Taylor's book, new developments in physics – Einstein's relativity theory and quantum mechanics – suggested that at the extremes of space and time, from the universe in its entirety to subatomic particles, the laws of Newtonian physics broke down. And more recently, scientists have extended that message of uncertainty and unpredictability to the everyday world.

Whether we are talking about stock markets, computer networks, or biological organisms, individual parts only make sense when we remember that they are part of larger wholes. And perhaps more importantly, those wholes can take on behaviors that are strikingly different from those of their pieces.

Thanks to this revolutionary perspective, we can finally transcend the limits of reductionism and discover crucial new ideas. As Donnella Meadows puts it:

> Let's face it. The universe is messy. It is nonlinear, turbulent, and chaotic. It is dynamic. It spends its time in transient behavior on its way to somewhere else, not in mathematically neat equilibria. It self-organizes and evolves. It creates diversity, not uniformity. That's what makes the world interesting, that's what makes it beautiful, and that's what makes it work.

The Diffusion of Cause and Effect

Nineteenth-century physics, based on Newton's laws of motion, posited a neat correspondence between cause and effect.

Scientists have concluded that this and many others of science's traditional assumptions about the way nature operates are fundamentally wrong. Far from being as predictable as clockwork, nature appears as random as a throw of the dice.

Unintended Consequences

Some of the many unintended effects of reductionism in organizations include: silos, poor communication, inadequate levels of cooperation and collaboration, waste, rework, and insufficient organizational capability to support strategy.

Limiting Initiative

Inherent in the command-and-control paradigm is the idea that a person or few people in charge give the solution, that it is the only solution, to other people who are in charge of implementing it. Thus the organization is heavily dependent upon the limited cognitive and information-processing capabilities of a few individuals at the top of the hierarchy. This reduces the capacity for the majority of the organization's members to take the initiative, act autonomously, and respond to local-level information.

The End of Stability

The reductionist model to organization is built on the axiom of a relatively static system in a relatively static environment. The primary focus of this form of control is to remove surprise, to dampen down change, and keep an organization moving stably through time according to the prior intentions of its members. All of these features mean that these systems are resistant to change, innovation, and evolution, and are thus inept at dealing with the dynamic and volatile environment we face today.

Local Solutions Lead to Global Problems

The best way to understand this is the physician's single, focused approach toward short-term relief. Treating high blood pressure by prescribing diuretics will impact your kidneys. But hey, the doctor responsible for blood pressure isn't the same person responsible for your kidneys, so it's not their problem. Wise physicians know that treating the whole person is far more helpful to a patient's well-being.

So when reductionism is applied to anything other than locally contained situations – that is, when applied to complex systems – it will actually create far more problems than the solution of the moment it is intended to address. Placing all one's energy toward minimizing the one cause or maximizing an isolated outcome will ultimately result in the destruction of the system itself.

Reductionism Diminishes Understanding

Because a system is a set of relationships – deeply nested interdependent relationships – every action will affect multiple relationships throughout the system. Moreover, one action has multiple effects and those effects are non-local and non-linear. Understanding the emergent properties of the system cannot be realized by breaking things apart. Reductionism as an approach to managing systems diminishes understanding and thus reduces the soundness of decisions.

The Limits of Closed Systems

One reason Newtonian models were so successful in predicting was because they only considered systems, such as the planetary system, that are essentially closed. Open systems, on the other hand, depend on a much larger and more complex environment than the system itself, so that its effect can never be truly controlled or predicted.

The Feeling of Isolation

If you are treated like a cog in a wheel, you feel lost in the organizations of which you are a part.

"When asked what they do for a living," Peter Senge writes in *The Fifth Dimension,*

> most people describe the tasks they perform every day, not the purpose of the greater enterprise in which they take part. Most see themselves within a "system" over which they have little or no influence. They "do their job," put in their time, and try to cope with the forces outside of their control.

The Inability to Explain Emergence

The concept that is hardest to explain with a reductionist point of view is that of emergent phenomenon.

The Newtonian perspective assumes that all can be explained by the careful examination of the parts. Yet that does not work for many aspects of human behavior. We have all experienced situations in which the whole is not the sum of the parts – where we cannot explain the outcomes of a situation by studying the individual elements.

For example, when a natural disaster strikes a community, we have seen spontaneous organization where there is no obvious leader, controller, or designer. In these contexts, we find that groups of people create outcomes and have impacts which are far greater than would have been predicted by summing up the resources and skills available within the group. In these cases there is self-organization in which outcomes emerge which are highly dependent on the relationships and context rather than merely the parts. Stuart Kauffman calls this "order for free" and Kevin Kelly refers to it as "creating something out of nothing".

A whirlpool is a phenomenon that is hard to explain by breaking down into component parts. Instead, the whirlpool depends in a non-trivial way on the shape of the riverbed that the water is flowing over. It is even hard to describe the exact edge where a whirlpool stops and the regular river begins.

In the nineteenth century some phenomena, like turbulence, were believed to be caused by the "breakdown" of the normal rules. Somehow, the simple rules exist to a point, and then the rules stop applying.

Why has the Current Paradigm been so Dominant?

The robustness and endurance of the machine as the predominant metaphor of the 20th century management practice is nothing short of amazing given the mounting evidence that it doesn't work.

Jon Hegel

Our problem in making sense of today when all is complex is that for many of us these are the only skills we have:

Most of us are taught, from a young age, that in order to solve a problem, we simply need to break it down to its core components and solve for x. We learn science experiments that have an aim, method and outcome, a linear process from problem to solution. We are socialized to respond to reward and punishment and by the time we have graduated from 15 to 20+ years of institutionalized education, we have trained our brains to think in clear, ordered and, yes, very linear ways. The problem with this is that the world is not linear. Whilst life may be marked by a start and an end, by birth and death, it is most certainly not a straight ordered line; it is a chaotic mess of experiences that make and define our understanding of the world.

Linear thinking is reductionist, it's all about breaking things down and reducing complexity into manageable order. But the by-product of reductionist thinking, is that we are very quick to solve a problem with the same thinking that led to its cause. This, according to Einstein, is not the way to solve problems – instead, it just leads to more problems.

Leyla Acaroglu, Medium

Note

1. *eXtreme Project Management: Using Leadership, Principles, and Tools to Deliver Value in the Face of Volatility*, Douglas DeCarlo, John Wiley & Sons.

Chapter 2

The Paradigm Shifts

The alternative is to stop seeing an organization as a machine, and to begin viewing it as a kind of living organism. This requires a holistic approach that reflects chaos theory's focus on the overall behavior of a system. Living systems have integrity. Their character depends on the whole. The same is true for organizations; to understand the most challenging managerial issues requires seeing the whole system that generates the issues.

Peter Senge, The Fifth Discipline

If you want to get a quantum leap increase in project production you have to think differently, kill a lot of sacred cows, and implement different tooling.

A dramatic improvement in project production is not going to happen without a significant paradigm shift.

Shifting a paradigm means leaving behind everything your past worldview was based on. This means changing at a core level and accepting that what you believed to be true might not apply anymore in this new paradigm.

Shifting the Paradigm

You don't see something until you have the right metaphor to let you perceive it.

James Gleick, Chaos: Making a New Science

Paradigm shifts are critical to ground-breaking change.

By definition, we believe the existing paradigm to be the right one and therefore cannot imagine anything other than that at that point of time. If you think that something functions like a machine, your solutions will be based on building or fixing the machine. We just operate under that paradigm and try to optimize it. At some point, however, we cannot get better within the paradigm anymore. That's why, for example, all project management systems look the same. Sure, they have some differences, but it's more like painting lipstick on a pig. It's still a pig.

This is when we are given a choice: we can either accept that we reached the end of the line and stay within that paradigm. Or we can shift the paradigm.

Paradigms are the single most determining factor for any and every outcome.

Killing Sacred Cows

> It's the best possible time to be alive, when almost everything you thought you knew is wrong.
>
> *Tom Stoppard, Arcadia, Act 1, Scene four*

To shift a paradigm, we need to question the underlying assumptions that support the paradigm and replace them with something that is more likely to give us the results we are looking for. This requires killing the sacred cows upon which traditional project management is based, and indeed, by establishing a different mindset or worldview. If your worldview is based on the assumption that the earth is flat, you would think twice about setting off on an ocean voyage for fear of falling off the edge. You need to change your basic assumptions to change the outcome.

For example, does spending time developing a detailed plan make sense when we *know* things are going to change? Instead of constantly scheduling and re-scheduling task deadlines, what if we do away with them altogether? What if we eliminate the need to match resources with constantly changing schedules and priorities, like playing a game of Tetris? What if we dispensed with Gantt charts, a 100-plus-year-old invention designed for a different time and a different purpose, as a way to plan and manage projects? What if we recognize that percent complete is a subjective, backward-looking metric that isn't much better than a set of random numbers?

Only by asking questions like these will we be able to shift the paradigm that governs how we currently manage work in the enterprise, and replace it with a radically different solution that is much better suited to the needs of the twenty-first-century organization.

A New Paradigm

New business models like Uber and AirBnB show us that the most efficient operations behave like Complex Adaptive Systems (CAS), where self-managing participants, following a set of simple rules, organize themselves to solve incredibly complex problems.

Uber is the perfect example of a company which understood that simply tweaking the way things were being done in their industry would not be able to meet the needs and possibilities of their marketplace. Therefore, Uber looked at how it could shift the paradigm by taking a radically different approach.

Instead of trying to function like a "well-oiled machine" where things "work like clockwork", Uber functions more like a living organism. It fully embraces characteristics of a CAS.

With Uber, order does not come about as a result of careful planning and effective execution, but rather from the inherent capacity of living systems to find new forms of order.

Uber was able to:

■ eliminate the need for centralized command and control;
■ make transactions between providers and consumers frictionless;
■ make onboarding of providers and customers effortless;
■ eliminate the need for complicated regulations to govern collective behavior;
■ make scheduling irrelevant;
■ keep the amount of management oversight needed to a bare minimum.

It did this by creating a platform that allows self-managing participants, following a set of simple rules, to organize themselves to provide the best service possible to its consumers.

Changing the Paradigm

Our Newtonian worldview has led us to focus our efforts on how to get the machine called an organization to work efficiently. Machines are exactly the wrong metaphor for what we need, since machines have no intelligence – they simply follow the instructions given to them, and only work in the specific conditions predicted by their engineers. Changes in their environment wreak havoc because they have no capacity to adapt.

But if we change our thought paradigm, we will start asking a different set of questions and think of different kinds of solutions. If organizations are living systems, then they have many innate capacities, and we need to learn to harness them.

If you change the way you look at things, the things you look at change.

A dramatic improvement in project production is not going to happen without a significant paradigm shift.

Shifting a paradigm means leaving behind everything your past worldview was based on. This means changing at a core level and accepting that what you believed to be true might not apply anymore in this new paradigm.

In the project management world, for example, this includes questioning the assumptions that:

- Gantt charts are an appropriate tool for planning and managing projects;
- the best way to ensure that a project will finish on time is to try to make every task finish on time;
- the sooner a project is initiated, the sooner it will be completed;
- percent complete is the right way to measure progress;
- resources should be fully utilized at all times;
- if we plan in more detail, we'll get better results (and/or reduce uncertainty).

Systems Thinking

The first movement away from Newtonianism and Scientific Management came with the emergence of Systems Thinking.

What is a System?

The first challenge is to define what a system is.

> A system is a set of related components that work together in a particular environment to perform whatever functions are required to achieve the systems objective.
>
> *Donella Meadows, Thinking in Systems*

What is Systems Thinking?

Systems Thinking is a way of seeing the world as a series of interconnected and interdependent systems rather than lots of independent parts. As a thinking tool, it seeks to oppose the reductionist view – the idea that a system can be understood by the sum of its isolated parts – and replace it with expansionism, the view that everything is part of a larger whole and that the connections between all elements are critical.

Seeing things in this way helps create a more flexible view of the world and the way it works, and it illuminates opportunities for addressing some of its existing and evolving problem arenas.

Systems Thinking is the process of understanding how things, regarded as systems, influence one another within a whole, and that the only way to fully understand a problem is to understand the parts in relation to the whole.

Take a bicycle, for example. A bicycle is made up of parts, such as chains, wheels, and so on, and these parts are put together or organized in a specific way so as to make them function as a vehicle of transportation.

The human body is highly organized through a complex set of relations between its parts. Out of the arrangement of these parts in a specific way we get the overall functioning of a living organism. Because the parts are so strongly defined by their connections and function within the body as an entirety, to properly describe the parts we need to first understand the functioning of the whole body.

Essential properties are unchanged whether	Changed if you take away pieces or add more pieces, If you cut the system in half you do
The parts are not connected and can	Its behavior depends on the total structure
Its behavior (if any) depends on its size	

Like the story of the blind men and the elephant, the behavior of a system cannot be known just by knowing the elements of which the system is made.

This approach to describing things through understanding their place within the function of the whole of which they are a part is called synthesis, and synthesis is the foundations of systems thinking.

Elements of Systems Thinking

- Every system is an interconnected set of elements which is coherently organized in a way that achieves a purpose. There is a set of necessary conditions that must be satisfied to maximize the achievements of that goal.
- Systems live or die as integrated systems, *not* as a collection of discrete, independent components. A system cannot be understood simply as the sum of its parts.

■ Every system is made up of many subsystems and is itself a part of larger systems. Just as we are made up of atoms with molecules and quantum particles, problems are made up of problems within problems. Every system is like a Matryoshka doll, made up of smaller and smaller parts within a larger whole.

■ A vision of the future is set in advance, an assessment of the present informs you about the current state, and the gap between future vision and current reality generates a creative tension which inspires action. The aim is to start by getting "the full picture".

■ Since everything is interconnected, there are constant feedback loops and flows between elements of a system. We can observe, understand, and intervene in feedback loops once we understand their type and dynamics.

■ Causality is about deciphering the way things influence each other in a system. Understanding causality leads to a deeper perspective on agency, feedback loops, connections, and relationships, which are all fundamental parts of systems mapping.

■ Systems mapping identifies and maps the elements of "things" within a system to understand how they interconnect, relate, and act in a complex system, and from here, unique insights and discoveries can be used to develop interventions, shifts, or policy decisions that will dramatically change the system in the most effective way.

What Happens When You Saw a Cow in Half?

Here is an example to help you get into the systems mindset: Say you have a glass of milk. If you add more milk to it, you'll end up with a larger amount of milk. On the other hand, if you have a cow who produces milk and you add a new cow to the other one, you won't get a larger cow – you'll get two cows who can produce more milk. If you pour half of the milk into another glass, you have two separate glasses of milk.

If you cut a cow in half, you don't get two cows – in this case the system (the cow!) is dramatically changed, and the cow is no longer able to produce milk. Cut the cow in half, and you'll have two heaps of meat, not two cows. This is because systems function as a whole and "heaps" do not.

The critical thing to know here is that systems are dramatically affected by changes within subsystems. After all, everything is interconnected in a system, and we live in one gigantic eco-system that sustains life on Earth through its interrelationships, creating the right environment for the grass to grow to feed the cow that makes the milk.

Draper L. Kauffman, Jr., Systems One:
An Introduction to Systems Thinking

Conclusion

Ultimately, approaching things from a systems perspective is about tackling big, messy, real-world problems rather than isolating cause and effect down to a single point. In the latter case, "solutions" are often just Band-Aids (that may cause unintended consequences) as opposed to real and holistic systemic solutions. Looking for the links and relationships within the bigger picture helps identify the systemic causes and lends itself to innovative, more holistic ideas and solutions.[1]

Chaos Theory

The real advance against reductionism found mathematical basis with the work of chaos theory, which demonstrated that no breakdown is necessary, but showed how regular iterative interactions can produce both smooth and complex phenomena. This brought about researchers in the field of complexity, to ponder the nature of complexity, and why it is that it does not yield to reduction.

"Chaos theory" is the general term for this new model of how things work. In the early 1960s, Edward Lorenz developed a computer program that simulated a weather system. By plugging in numbers representing the initial state of winds and temperatures, Lorenz's program churned out the subsequent weather pattern as it evolved over time. Lorenz, like most scientists, assumed that small changes in the initial conditions he fed into the computer would result in correspondingly small changes in the evolution of the entire system. To his surprise, he discovered that even the most minuscule of changes caused drastic alterations in the weather pattern. In effect, a slight breeze in Idaho or a one-degree drop in temperature in Massachusetts could end up changing balmy weather in Florida into a hurricane a month later.

The effect defied both intuition and what meteorologists had previously understood about their science.

This basic insight – that minute changes can lead to radical deviations in the behavior of a natural system – has inaugurated an equally radical shift in how scientists see the world. Put simply, the nineteenth-century emphasis on predictability and control has given way to a late twentieth-century appreciation for the power of randomness and chance. For all practical purposes, the behavior of even relatively simple physical systems is fundamentally unpredictable.

This is summed up succinctly by the character Ian Malcolm, in Michael Crichton's book *Jurassic Park*:

> [We] have soothed ourselves into imagining sudden change as something that happens outside the normal order of things. An accident, like a car crash. Or beyond our control, like a fatal illness. We do not conceive of sudden, radical, irrational change as built into the very fabric of existence. Yet it is.
>
> And chaos theory teaches us that straight linearity, which we have come to take for granted in everything from physics to fiction, simply does not exist. Linearity is an artificial way of viewing the world.
>
> Real life isn't a series of interconnected events occurring one after another like beads strung on a necklace. Life is actually a series of encounters in which one event may change those that follow in a wholly unpredictable, even devastating way.

But this is not to say that chaotic systems don't have any patterns. While the idea that nature is fundamentally random is counter-intuitive, chaos theory's second basic insight is even more so: that patterns do lurk beneath the seemingly random behavior of these systems. In fact, systems don't end up just anywhere; certain paths apparently make more sense – or at least occur much more frequently – and chaos theorists call such paths "strange attractors".

We actually find hidden regularities within the complex variety of a system's behavior. That's why chaos has now become a very broad theory that is used to study everything from the stock market, to rioting crowds, to brain waves during epilepsy – any sort of complex system where there is confusion and unpredictability. We can find an underlying order. An underlying order is essentially characterized by the movement of the system within phase space.

Thus, while meteorologists cannot say with certainty what the weather will be on a particular day in the future, they can estimate the probability of the kind of weather likely to occur. In other words, strange attractors allow scientists to determine within broad statistical parameters what a system is likely to do – but never exactly when a system is likely to do it.

The cause-and-effect precision of traditional physics has been replaced by the statistical estimate of probabilities.

In addition, the way scientists identify the predictable patterns in a system has been turned on its head. Instead of trying to break down a system into its component parts and analyze the behaviors of those parts independently – the reductionist tradition that so influenced Taylor – many scientists have had to learn a more holistic approach. They focus increasingly on the dynamics of the overall system. Rather than attempting to explain how order is designed into the parts of a system, they now emphasize how order emerges from the interaction of those parts as a whole.

Complexity Science

> Complexity theory does not embrace the radical holism of systems theory, the notion that everything matters and everything has to be taken into account.
>
> *Steven Phelan, What is complexity science, really?*

The quest to gain insight into and make use of the order that emerges from chaotic systems leads us to Complexity Science.

While Systems Thinking seeks to define an ideal future and then define strategies to "close the gap", Complexity Science works with the evolutionary potential of the present, i.e. it seeks to understand the "now", find out what can be changed (in a measurable way), and then take small evolutionary steps in a more positive direction without any assumption of the end destination.

Systems Theory deals with "complicated" systems: there are input and output flows and straightforward cause and effect (as in machines) where the pieces can be understood in isolation and the whole can be reassembled from the parts. One problem can bring down the system, since complicated systems cannot adapt.

Systems Thinking versus Complexity Thinking

Factor	Systems Thinking	Complexity Thinking
Ideal future vs. evolutionary potential of the present	Systems thinking seeks to define an ideal future (e.g. culture) and then define strategies to "close the gap".	Complexity works with the evolutionary potential of the present, i.e. it seeks to understand the "now", find out what can be changed (in a measurable way), and then take small evolutionary steps in a more positive direction without any assumption of the end destination.
Complex systems are modulated, not driven	Change one thing, and the other components of the system remain unchanged.	Change one thing, and the other components in the system change as well – in ways that don't repeat.
Complex systems are dispositional, not causal	You can accurately predict the behavior of the system (can see cause and effect).	One can observe tendency or propensity for the system to move in a general direction. As we move in any given direction by making choices (and per definition closing off opportunities as we make these choices), there will always be a certain fluidity, not a direct path as in a causal system.

continued

Continued

Factor	Systems Thinking	Complexity Thinking
Extrinsic rewards destroy intrinsic motivation	Setting explicit outcome-based targets with associated incentives destroys intrinsic motivation (i.e. people start chasing the target without considering potential consequences). Another way to put it: Anything explicit will be gamed. Setting explicit targets (ideal behavior) and attempting to "close the gap" simply leads to gaming behavior and unintended consequences.	In complex systems we try to measure individuals based on the outcome of the project.
People are not widgets, nor are they ants	Systems thinking often seeks to "engineer" an ideal culture, which in essence means "engineering" people and their interactions. A symptom of this is how consultants and leaders seem to disregard the impact of constant re-structuring – moving people around as if they really are interchangeable widgets.	Complexity acknowledges that people have agency; that we have multiple identities that we switch between seamlessly (e.g. I can be wife, daughter, entrepreneur, friend, and different identities may have different thinking patterns based on priorities). Bottom line: People aren't cogs in a machine, nor are they ants or birds.

Complicated vs. Complex: An Alternate Reality

Complexity is a given in today's world and it is increasing every day. To gain a competitive advantage in this ever more competitive environment, companies need to master complexity.

Boston Consulting Group

The paradigm shift starts with understanding the difference between something that is complicated and something that is complex.

Complexity is a word that is thrown around a lot, but surprisingly few people understand what it really means and how it differs from something that is complicated.

Knowing the difference between something that is complex versus something that is complicated is one of the keys to better project management. Treating complex problems as if they are complicated is a sure-fire recipe for failure.

An Alternate Reality

There are two contrasting worldviews. On the one hand, there is the "mechanical" view of the world, the idea that the world works like a machine. In this view the future is a predetermined path inexorably unfolding from the present. We can analyze the facts, predict the future, decide how to intervene, make and execute plans and control and measure outcomes. The world can be understood by breaking it down into constituent parts, and these can be dealt with in piecemeal fashion. There is no learning, variety, adaptation, innovation or surprise.

This pervasive mechanical worldview maintains its attraction as it provides a sense of order, purpose and control. It makes analyses tractable. It underpins processes of management and policy making and it defines, for many, how they view their role in the world, and shapes how they engage with life and work.

In contrast a complexity worldview sees the world as essentially interconnected and rich with forms and patterns that have been shaped by history and context. A complexity worldview reminds us of the limits to certainty, it emphasizes that things are in a continual process of "becoming" and that there is potential for startlingly new futures where what emerges can be unexpected and astonishing.

*Jean Boulton, Peter Allen and Cliff Bowman, Embracing
Complexity: Strategic Perspectives for an Age of Turbulence*

Complicated Systems

A complicated system is one in which the components can be separated and dealt with in a systematic and logical way based on rules and algorithms. It may be hard to see, but there's a fixed order in something that is merely complicated and that allows you to deal with it in a repeatable manner.

Complicated systems require more expertise in their management, but as long as the proper expertise is available and used, the attractiveness of complicated systems is that they can generally be successfully managed. It is simply a matter of making sure that the proper models are being used for the situation at hand.

Complicated systems are all fully predictable. For example, the wiring on an aircraft is complicated. To figure out where everything goes would take a long time. But if you studied it for long enough, you could know with (near) certainty what each electrical circuit does and how to control it. The system is ultimately knowable. If understanding it is important, the effort to study it and make a detailed diagram of it would be worthwhile.

Complex Systems

On the other hand, a complex system is one in which you cannot get a firm handle on the parts, and there are no rules, algorithms, or natural laws. Things that are complex have no such degree of order, control, or predictability. A complex system is much more challenging – and different – than the sum of its parts, because its parts interact in unpredictable ways.

Managing people is a complex challenge. So is integrating the two merging companies or figuring out how the market will react to a new product or strategy. Maybe you'll get lucky and figure it out once, but whatever you did this time won't generate the same result next time.

Complex systems are nuanced and require a nuanced approach. The one thing that will not work is a rigid, rules-based, complicated approach. Complex systems defy attempts to be created in an engineering effort, and the components in the system co-evolve through their relationships with other components.

Example

Complicated	Complex
Sending a rocket to the moon	Raising a child
Rigid protocols or formulas are needed	Rigid protocols have a limited application or are counter-productive
Sending one rocket increases the likelihood that the next one will also be a success	Raising one child provides experience but is no guarantee of success with the next
High levels of expertise and training in a variety of fields are necessary for success	Expertise helps but only when balanced with responsiveness to the particular child
Key elements of each rocket must be identical for success	Every child is unique and must be understood as an individual
There is a high degree of certainty of outcome	Uncertainty of outcome remains
Success depends on a blueprint that directs both the development of separate parts and specifies the exact relationship in which to assemble them	Cannot separate the parts from the whole; essence exists in the relationships between different people, experiences, different moments of time
For example, in a project management context, the creation of the project plan – sequence of tasks, predecessors and successors – is complicated. There may be different ways to do it, but with the right expertise it can be done, and the result will be approximately the same every time (i.e. for repetitive projects).	For example, in a project management context, the management of resources across multiple projects is complex. There are many ways to do this, but there is no way to create certainty because there are so many uncertain and interrelated variables, and the outcome will be different every time.

Why Is This Important?

The two ways of thinking involve different mindsets, different expectations, and different tolerances of ambiguity. They involve different attributes and skills. They require dramatically different management techniques.

Rick Nason, It's not complicated:
The Art and Science of Complexity in Business

This could be dismissed as an exercise in semantics, except for one thing: when facing a problem, managers tend to automatically default to complicated thinking. Instead, they should be "consciously managing complexity".

As Nason points out in his book, solutions to complicated problems don't work well with complex problems. Complex problems involve too many unknowns and too many interrelated factors to reduce to rules and processes.

It's like trying to fit a square peg in a round hole. Indeed, attempting to solve a complex problem with a complicated solution could result in perverse behaviors leading to poor complex outcomes.

- Complicated thinking leads managers to think that they are doing something purposeful when in reality they are not, and in fact they are likely doing more harm than good. We try to design, specify, impose, dictate when we should be designing, enabling, intervening, stabilizing. The former is a different skill set and has a different set of tools from the latter.
- Complicated thinkers tend to get too intellectually invested in an idea and refuse to let go, despite sometimes overwhelming evidence that the plan is not working. Complexity thinkers have the humility and flexibility not to get trapped into this low-probability strategy.
- Complexity thinkers understand that it is all about the creation of a context that enables the emergence of the desired outcomes. We may not be able to intervene or directly control the outcome to events but we can manage the initial conditions, the tools, protocols, and connections, all of which influence the context within which the organization's elements generate outcomes.
- Complexity implies that there is a level of control available; but it is not complete control, and the situation is not completely manageable. This mode of management can be quite stressful if the manager has a complicated mindset that abhors ambiguity and uncertainty.

Example: Fighting Al Qaeda in a Complex World

General Stanley McChrystal learned the hard way that fighting a war in a complex environment requires an approach that is quite different from one used in a less complex environment:

The Al Qaeda in Iraq (AQI) that our Task Force confronted in 2004 looked on the surface like a traditional insurgency. But under the surface it operated unlike anything we had seen before. In place of a traditional hierarchy, it took the form of a dispersed network that proved devastatingly effective against our objectively mere qualified force.

AQI's unorthodox structure allowed it to thrive in an operating environment that diverged radically from what we had traditionally faced: the twenty-first century is more connected, faster paced, and less predictable than previous eras. Though we encountered this shift on the battlefield similar changes are affecting almost every sector of society.

To win we had to change. Surprisingly, that change was less about tactics or new technology than it was about the internal architecture and culture or our force – in other words, our approach to management.

Complexity produces a fundamentally different situation from the complicated challenges of the past; complicated problems required great effort, but ultimately yielded to prediction. Complexity means that, in spite of our increased abilities to track and measure, the world has become, in many ways, vastly less predictable.

This unpredictability is fundamentally incompatible with reductionist managerial models based around planning and prediction. The new environment demands a new approach.

Although we intuitively know the world has changed, most leaders reflect a model and leader development process that are sorely out of date. We often demand unrealistic levels of knowledge in leaders and force them into ineffective attempts to micro-manage.

The temptation to lead as a chess master, controlling each move of the organization, must give way to an approach as a gardener, enabling rather than directing.

> *General Stanley McChrystal, US Army, Team of Teams:*
> *New Rules of Engagement for a Complex World*

Beware: The Reluctance to Embrace Complexity Thinking

> Our aversion to uncertainty is deep and primordial. It implies the lack of control that is required for our survival, it signals danger.
>
> *Joss Colchester, Complexity Labs*

Unfortunately, there is a lot of resistance to embracing complexity. Why is this?

Complicated Solutions are Appealing

> Given managers' desire for control, complexity is far from a convenient reality. Rather than face the brutal reality of the system they are working to sustain, managers often work in silos, creating models and mechanisms that impose a veneer of certainty.
>
> *BBVA INNOVATION, Order from Chaos: How to Apply Complexity Theory at Work*

We often implicitly describe complex problems as complicated, and hence employ solutions that are wedded to rational planning approaches. These often lead to inappropriate solutions because they neglect many aspects of complexity. This is like the old joke about the drunk who is stumbling around near a lamp post. He is asked what he is doing and he says he is looking for his car keys:

> "Oh, where do you think you lost them?" "Down the block near my car," he says. "So why are you looking for them here?" "Because the light is better."

The sophistication of our models, theories, and language for complicated problems can be as seductive as the lamplight. They provide better "light" and clarity, and yet can lead to investigations that are ill-equipped to address Complex Adaptive Systems. We still attempt to cure problems in complex systems with a naïve understanding of cause and effect.

It is easier to spend time refining a blueprint than it is to accept that there is much uncertainty about what action is required and what outcomes will be achieved. When dealing with a complex system, it is better to conduct a range of smaller innovations and find ways to constantly evaluate and learn from the results and adjust the next steps rather than to work to a set plan.[2]

Complex Solutions aren't Convenient

According to an article entitled "Why Managers Haven't Embraced Complexity" by Richard Straub in the *Harvard Business Review*:

> Complexity theory has been around for a few decades, but has not lead to major changes in management practices.
>
> There are, I think, a few major reasons that it didn't – and that also suggest that the overdue change might now finally take place.
>
> Complexity isn't a convenient reality given managers' desire for control.
>
> The promise of applying complexity science to business has undoubtedly been held up by managers' reluctance to see the world as it is. Where complexity exists, managers have always created models and mechanisms that wish it away. It is much easier to make decisions with fewer variables and a straightforward understanding of cause-and-effect.
>
> The recognition of complexity is at its core a view of the world that that makes us more humble and more open. It is the awareness that too often our interventions will not achieve what we wanted and we will be shocked by unintended consequences. At the same time, it is the acknowledgement that simplistic "can do" thinking and linear approaches in organizations and markets, which are by definition complex, won't be sufficient. And it is the prod to us to better understand why.
>
> Managers, I think, should now get ready to face the full complexity of their organizations and economic environments and, if not control them, learn how to intervene with deliberate, positive effect. Embracing complexity will not make their jobs easier, but it is a recognition of reality, and an idea whose time has come.

Summary

In project management, it's much easier to spend time creating and maintain a detailed schedule than it is to spend time helping to make sure things are done as quickly as possible. We know task deadlines are always going to change – and yet we persist in creating artificial deadlines.

Sidebar: Old Paradigm/New Paradigm

If you are wearing a Newtonian hat and using a Newtonian compass to navigate your way through a Quantum world, you are likely to feel frustrated and under stress most of the time. You are suffering from Newtonian Neurosis. You will not be at ease. You will suffer from dis-ease because your actions are in conflict with reality. And, reality rules, but only 100 percent of the time.

Byron Katie, Loving What Is[3]

Traditional Paradigm	New Paradigm
Stability is the norm	Chaos is the norm
The world is linear and predictable	Uncertainty reigns
Seek to minimize change	Welcomes change
Work plans are "frozen"	Work plans are never complete
Work plans are rigid and self-preserving	Work plans are adaptable, flexible
Participant behavior is controlled	Participant creativity is encouraged
Managers use command and-control	Managers use attractors and define boundaries
The plan is used to drive results	Results are used to drive planning
Establish strong procedures and policies	Agree on guidelines, principles and values
Correct to the original baseline	Correct to what is possible
Projects are machines to be kept on track	Projects are a living organism that emerges
Projects deliver on the planned result	Projects deliver on the discovered result

By considering project management (other than planning) as complex can help deal with them, as many of what are usually identified as "problems" to be controlled and avoided (uncertainty, variability, conflicts) are just evidence of a complex nature.

Notes

1. The Critical Difference between Complex and Complicated. https://sloan review.mit.edu/article/the-critical-difference-between-complex-and-complicated/.
2. Complicated or complex – knowing the difference is important, Learning for sustainability.
3. *eXtreme Project Management™: The What & Why, Doug DeCarlo*, www. projectconnections.com/articles/040203-decarlo.html.

Chapter 3

Complex Adaptive Systems (CAS) Theory

> The mistake of modern science is to pretend that everything is a clock. ... But that approach is doomed to failure. We live in a universe not of clocks but of clouds.
>
> *Jonah Lehrer, Imagine: How Creativity Works*

Complexity Science provides a framework to study systems that display perplexing behaviors if looked at through the lens of traditional thinking. What might appear chaotic may really be progressive and adaptive. And what might have been seen to be good because it was stable, orderly, and predictable may in fact be evidence of an impending death spiral.

Complexity Science provides the language, the metaphors, the conceptual frameworks, the models, and the theories which help make the idiosyncrasies non-idiosyncratic and the illogical logical.

Understanding CAS concepts allows us to think more innovatively about solutions in general. Adopting a different frame of reference changes one's perspective so that what was remote and unnatural becomes sensible and natural.

If we view project management as a Complex Adaptive System, then knowledge of CAS learned elsewhere can be applied to drive a new philosophy of project management.

What is a CAS?

More than 60 years ago, scientists knew that Newton was wrong about the way the world worked. It turns out that we do not live in an even remotely linear world; in fact, our world should be categorized as non-linear. But despite the fact that the machine metaphor has been all but abandoned by twentieth-century science, project management methodologies continue to clutch the reassuring image of a clockwork system. We have to come to grips with the fact that we are not cogs in a timepiece, but integral participants in a distinctly living, growing, and ever-changing whole being – what scientists call a Complex Adaptive System.

Over the past two or three decades, scientists have explored living systems in many fields – as diverse as biology and economics – to search for common properties that explain complex phenomena such as Darwinian natural selection and increasing returns on the stock market. They have uncovered the knowledge that that many natural systems (brains, immune systems, ecologies, societies) and many artificial systems (parallel and distributed computing systems, artificial intelligence systems, artificial neural networks, evolutionary programs) are characterized by complex behaviors that emerge as a result of interactions among their component systems at different levels of organization.

These results have been used to unravel the mysteries of the collective behavior of living systems in nature such as the flocking of birds, schooling of fish, marching of ants, and swarming of bees for strategic purposes.

While the individual "agents" in these groups possess only local strategic rules and capacity, their collective behavior is characterized by an overlaying order, self-organization, and a collective intelligence that is greater than the sum of the parts. In addition, these living systems regularly display a remarkable ability to adapt to a complex and dynamic environment.[1]

Definition

Systems Theory deals with "complicated" systems: there are input and output flows and straightforward cause and effect (as in machines) where the pieces can be understood in isolation and the whole can be reassembled from the parts. One problem can bring down the system, since complicated systems cannot adapt.

Complex Adaptive Systems, on the other hand, are adaptive (as in ecosystems, like the weather). Complex systems adapt to changes in their environment. Hence the "adaptive" in the name "Complex Adaptive Systems".

A Complex Adaptive System (CAS) is a system of semi-autonomous agents who have the freedom to act according to a set of simple rules in order to maximize a specific goal. A CAS is a highly adaptive, self-organizing, interrelated, interdependent, interconnected entity that behaves as a unified whole. It learns from experience and adjusts (not just reacts) to changes in the environment.

This theory can be demonstrated by what happens when a set of traffic lights at a busy junction cease to function. At first there is a lot of hesitancy, but gradually a pattern emerges which the motorists recognize and they all start to cross a few at a time in each direction; and, very often, what emerges is more effective than the normal pattern. This continues very well until in a complex world a cop arrives and starts to direct the traffic, and of course the queues build up and are worse than usual. The system is clearly quite complex as there are no set rules, but more importantly, it is adaptive in that the pattern changes as the circumstances change – hence a Complex Adaptive System.

Complex Adaptive Systems are all around us – the weather, the ant colonies, the stock market, our immune systems, the neighborhoods, the governments, the sporting events, and, most importantly, the organizations in which we work. The "participants" in every system exist and behave in total ignorance of the concept but that does not impede their contribution to the system. And every individual agent of a CA is itself a CAS: a tree, for example, is a CAS within a larger CAS (a forest) which is a CAS in a still larger CAS (an ecosystem).

The CAS way of thinking about and analyzing things is by recognizing complexity, patterns, and interrelationships rather than focusing on cause and effect. This allows policy makers, researchers – and project managers – to consider deeper underlying causes and interactions than may have been the case with more surface-level assumptions.

For example, complexity has improved understanding of world markets, ant colonies, traffic systems, urban planning, airline networks, seismology, virus research, etc. Conceiving these phenomena through a lens of complexity theory has provided a platform for new approaches, processes, and techniques.

The Properties of a CAS

> Never in the history of the world have we faced so much
> complexity combined with so much incompetence in
> understanding its properties.
>
> *Nassim Taleb, Black Swan*

CAS have a number of linked attributes or properties. Because the
attributes are all linked, it is impossible to identify the starting point for
the list of attributes. Each attribute can be seen to be both a cause and
effect of the other attributes. The attributes listed are all in stark contrast
to the implicit assumptions underlying traditional management and
Newtonian science.[2]

By understanding the fundamental properties of a CAS, you are able to
come up with solutions that work with the CAS rather than against it.

Self-organization

The idea of self-organization, or the spontaneous emergence of self-
maintaining order, is in direct contrast to a machine orientation of the world,
which assumes that the appearance of order requires the imposition of a
design from outside the system, just as an engineer designs and builds a
machine.[3]

Self-organization takes place through simple rules without a centralized
coordinator. No one is in complete control, and no one in the system has
complete information of it.

For managers, this means creating the *context* that facilitates the process
of self-organization to take place. We cannot directly control the outcome
of the system but we can influence the initial conditions. It's the grey area
between chaos and order – *chaordic*.

Like resilience, self-organization is often sacrificed for purposes of short-
term productivity and stability. Productivity and stability are the usual
excuses for turning a creative human being into a mechanical part of the
production process.

> **Traditional Management:** Get your ducks in a row
> **CAS-aware Management:** Self-organized ducks

Simple Rules

> Simple clear purpose and principles give rise to complex
> intelligent behaviors. Complex rules and regulations give rise to
> simple, stupid behaviors.
>
> *Dee Hock, Institutions in the Age of Marketing*

Simple rules provide a powerful weapon against the complexity. Simple rules guide complex collective behavior.

Complex Adaptive Systems are not complicated. The emerging patterns may have a rich variety, but like a kaleidoscope the rules governing the function of the system are quite simple.[4] Simple rules govern the interaction between agents. These rules determine how agents synchronize their state or cooperate.

This is completely counter-intuitive to conventional wisdom. We usually think that complex structures will only work if we have detailed blueprints or a comprehensive set of rules and regulations. While this is generally true for mechanical tasks, it is not the way the open systems of biology work.[5]

In the organic world, the secret to the effective execution of complex tasks is that order is created by the collaborative application of a few simple rules rather than by compliance with a complex set of controls. Thus, one of the distinguishing features of Complex Adaptive Systems is that responsibility for control and coordination rests with each of the individual participants rather than with one central executive.

So, while applying complicated solutions to complex problems is an understandable approach, the parts of a complex system can interact with one another in many different ways. This quickly overwhelms our ability to envision all possible outcomes.

> Simple Rules offers a fresh perspective on a fundamental question: How can people manage the complexity inherent in the modern world? Our answer, grounded in research and real-world results, is that simple rules tame complexity better than complicated solutions.
>
> By limiting the number of guidelines, simple rules help maintain a strict focus on what matters most while remaining easy to remember and use. In a wide range of decisions, simple rules can guide choice while leaving ample room to exercise judgment and creativity.
>
> *Don Sull and Kathy Eisenhardt, Simple Rules*

Example

If your project assignment is to get geese to fly in a "V" formation, how would you do it? The answer: set up a few rules that make it inherently beneficial for each goose:

- don't bump into each other;
- match up with the speed of the other geese flying nearby;
- replace the lead goose when it gets tired;
- always remain with the group.

A complex and efficient flying pattern emerges from these few simple rules.

This is in sharp contrast to how we build systems. Our goal is to impose as many rules as possible – so "exceptions" are kept to a minimum.

Attractors and Boundaries

> Managing flow in complex systems means you manage the emergence of beneficial coherence within attractors within boundaries. What you're looking to design is a working boundary that, with the right attractors, produces desired behaviors and outcomes.
>
> *Lecture by Dave Snowden, Embrace Complexity, Scale Agility*

In complex systems:

- An **attractor** is something that draws the system towards it.
- A **boundary** is something that contains the work (e.g. simple rules that ensure policies and procedures are followed).

When we see beneficial attractors – we attempt to stabilize and amplify them. When we see negative attractors – we attempt to dampen or destroy them.

David Snowden, who created Cynefin, a conceptual framework used to aid decision making, uses a child's birthday party to illustrate how attractors and boundaries work for managing self-organizing teams. You don't take a command-and-control approach to managing the birthday party, because you are not looking for a direct outcome. What you want is a self-organizing emergent outcome where people interact, and out of that interaction get the emergence of the children enjoying themselves.

So what needs to be done is to create the context that will induce the children to interact and self-organize. We put toys out, we make a little sports field out back where they can kick a ball around, we get a clown, some balloons, put some music on. **All of these attractors create the context**. You don't tell the children which ones to play with, but what you will see is that attractors will spontaneously form around some of the things and the children will be drawn into that for some time and, during that time, you will get the emergence of the fun party that you hoped for.

The other side of context setting are boundaries, or constraints. Boundaries do not have to be just physical or topological, but are primarily functional, behavioral, and communicational. Like making the garden the boundary of the party, and making inside the house out of bounds.

Non-linearity

We are often challenged by unintended system-level consequences arising from well-intentioned individual-level actions. The explanation lies in the concept of non-linearity.

In complex systems, there is a tenuous connection between cause and effect. Small changes can have huge effects. Alternatively, large changes may have little effect. Attempts to direct result in unintended consequences – the belief that more sophisticated systems will result in greater efficiency can have the opposite effect.

Non-linear effects arise when a small change in one aspect of a system results in a disproportionate response from the system. In other words, the small effort put into the system is magnified in its impact, giving rise to a larger or more energetic response than the effort initially put in to trigger the response.

Non-linearity and unpredictability proliferate because there is no simple relationship between cause and effect.

In these systems agents in the system adjust to every stimulus in ways that are not linear. That is, small input changes can produce large output changes. This is actually very encouraging, since it suggests that small inputs into a protracted or intractable conflict can conceivably produce large effects.[6]

Sensitivity to Initial Conditions

A deterministic system is a system that will produce the same results if you start with the same conditions. The outcome can be reliably predicted if you know the starting conditions. For example, if you fire a rifle several times at a target, the hits on the target will be closely grouped if all the initial conditions are almost identical.[7]

On the other hand, a CAS can produce wildly different results even if the starting conditions are almost exactly the same. If today's weather pattern is almost exactly the same as it was on a previous date, the weather a week later could be entirely different.

Sensitive dependence on initial conditions means that the further one goes into the future the more inaccurate predictions become. A consequence of sensitivity to initial conditions is that if we start with a limited amount of information about the system (as is usually the case in practice), then beyond a certain time the system is no longer predictable. Long-term and even some short-term predictions are meaningless in systems that are sensitive to initial conditions.

Weather systems are an obvious example of this phenomenon of non-linearity and sensitivity to initial conditions. This is also known as the *butterfly effect*, because it suggests that a butterfly that beats its wings in Peking today can transform a storm system next month in New York.

Requisite Variety

Minimal Variety. Until comparatively recently, organizations coped with environmental challenges mainly by measures to reduce the variety with which they had to cope. Mass production, for example, reduced the variety of its environment by limiting the range of choice available to consumers: product standardization was essentially an extrapolation of Henry Ford's slogan that customers could have the Model T in any color so long as it was black.[8]

Requisite Variety. The Law of Requisite Variety states that the system/person with the most flexibility of behavior will control the system – the greater the variety within the system the stronger it is.

If a system is to be able to deal successfully with the diversity of challenges that its environment produces, then it needs to have a repertoire of responses which is (at least) as nuanced as the problems thrown up by the environment. So a viable system is one that can handle the variability of its environment.[9]

This requires the ability to mass customize rather than mass produce. Organizations that retain minimal variety are no longer viable.

Resilience

Fragility. In a complicated system, if one piece, no matter how large or how small, breaks down, the entire system will break down. All parts, in this way, are essentially equally important. This means that if one link in the chain breaks the whole structure falls apart, putting the organization in a very precarious position.

Resilience. In a CAS, the failure of an element does not bring the whole system down. A CAS is able to adapt through things like modularity and self-organization. Resilience is a key factor in healthy, adaptive systems. Resilience is the capacity to absorb large amounts of disruptive change without a significant drop in quality or productivity

Sub-optimality

If you are building a bicycle and you leave one component out – like the chain – the bicycle ceases to operate. Therefore, it is critical in a complicated system to get everything just right, or else it won't work.

But a Complex Adaptive System does not have to be perfect in order for it to thrive within its environment. A solution doesn't have to be right, it just has to work. When it stops working, agents tinker their way into another solution.

Once it has reached the state of being good enough, *a Complex Adaptive System will trade off increased efficiency every time in favor of greater effectiveness.* Any energy used on being better than that is wasted energy. Yet we spend an inordinate amount of time trying to get the details right when it is unlikely to matter very much.

A flock of geese is a good example of sub-optimality. A V-shape is the most optimum way for the geese to fly, but spending the effort on making it less ragged isn't worth it.

Unlike a complicated system, if one part of the component stops working, the system can still function. If one duck drops out, the flock can continue on. Elements of the system are not equally important.

Distributed Control

CAS have distributed control rather than centralized control. Rather than having a command center which directs all of the agents, control is distributed throughout the system. In a school of fish, there is no "boss" which directs the other fishes' behavior. The independent agents (or fish) have the capacity to learn new strategies and adaptive techniques.

The coherence of a CAS's behavior relates to the interrelationships between the agents. You cannot explain the outcomes or behavior of a CAS from a thorough understanding of all of the individual parts or agents. The school of fish reacts to a stimulus (for example the threat of a predator) faster than any individual fish can react. The school has capacities and attributes which are not explainable by the capacities and attributes of the individual agents.

There is not one fish which is smarter than the others who is directing the school. If there was a smart "boss" fish, this form of centralized control would result in a school of fish reacting at least as slow as the fastest fish could respond. Centralized control would slow down the school's capacity to react and adapt.[10]

Emergence

Distributed control means that the outcomes of a CAS *emerge* from a process of self-organization rather than being designed and controlled externally or by a centralized body. The emergence is a result of the patterns of interrelationships between the agents. Emergence suggests unpredictability – an inability to state precisely how a system will evolve.

In a CAS, order emerges from the interaction of the independent participants. Order is not preordained before the work begins, but rather emerges through an iterative learning process.

While it often appears that the agents in a system interact in apparently random ways, patterns emerge. We see this all over nature – for example, a termite hill is a wondrous piece of architecture with a maze of interconnecting passages, large caverns, ventilation tunnels, and much more. Yet there is no grand plan, the hill just emerges as a result of the termites following a few simple local rules.[11]

In a similar way, as organizations go about their normal functions, patterns will begin to emerge – about customers, suppliers, and employees. Spotting these patterns early provides an advantage in terms of meeting customers' changing needs faster than competitors. Therefore, systems should evolve based on how people use them rather than being imposed from the top down.

Because CAS can quickly learn and adapt and are capable of efficiently aggregating the collective intelligence of their many participants, command and control is the wrong organizational structure when the primary business challenge is managing innovation.

Example: At a traffic intersection where the traffic lights suddenly stop working, patterns emerge from self-organization based on simple rules with sufficient feedback. Within a very short space of time, order is restored through self-organization of the drivers based on simple rules and feedback based on the cars moving into the intersection according to the established pattern. There is no command and control involved.

Feedback

Rapid feedback is critical to effective management in a complex environment. Feedback allows our plans to be imperfect at the start of a journey and quite good by the end. It gives us the data we need to adjust our planned route based on the actual territory encountered, rather than trudging forward blind with nothing but a map of what we thought the territory might look like.

A classic example given for illustrating feedback is a thermostat that regulates the temperature of a house. The system consists of a central controller where the desired temperature is set, a heater that creates an action that changes the state of the environment, and a sensor to feedback information about the environment to the controller. Wherever we have this basic degree of interaction and interdependence between elements, we can use the model of an adaptive system and feedback loops to describe its dynamics and thus we can model economies, society, and ecosystems in this way.

Nested Systems

Closed system. Most organizations think of themselves as closed systems. They believe that every agent and every aspect of the system is within their control, and that if something does go wrong the solution is also within their control. Again, in some rare cases this is true, but it is rarely a realistic mindset for an organization to have.

Open system. CAS are open systems, which means that there are inherently parts that are out of the organization's control – it is understood that not all elements can be controlled and therefore flexibility must be built into the system.[12]

All systems exist within their own environment, and they are also part of that environment. Therefore, as their environment changes, they need to co-evolve – change to ensure a best fit. But because they are part of their environment, when they change, they change their environment, and as it changes, they need to change again; and so it goes on as a constant process (that's why the most successful systems are ironically those that need to change most often). The systems we build today are not designed to be in constant flux – in fact, quite the opposite.

CAS are embedded or nested in other CAS. Each individual agent in a CAS is itself a CAS. In an ecosystem, a tree in a forest is a CAS and is also an agent in the CAS of the forest which is an agent in the larger ecosystem of the island, and so on. In health care, a doctor is a CAS and also an agent in the department which is a CAS and an agent in the hospital which is a CAS and an agent in health care which is a CAS and an agent in society. The agents co-evolve with the CAS of which they are a part.

Phase Transition

A phase transition takes place when some small change to a system causes a qualitative change in the system's state. Examples include the transition of ice to steam, the last drop of sand that causes the sand hill to collapse, the straw that breaks the camel's back.

Edge of Chaos

A system that is rigid isn't capable of rapidly responding to a changing environment, and will eventually die. In addition, nothing novel can be expected from systems that have high degrees of order and stability.

On the other hand, a system in chaos is too formless to coalesce, and ceases to function as a system. The most productive state to be in is at the "edge of chaos" where there is maximum variety and creativity, leading to new possibilities.

Complicated systems thrive and depend on order and control. But if any one broken chain can take the whole system down, it is imperative that no risks be taken. Risks can lead to rich rewards, which complicated systems do not allow for.

CAS thrive on the border between chaos and order. This means that while there must be some order for a system to function, total control cannot be imposed and chaos must thrive in small doses. Operating at the edge of chaos opens up avenues for disruptive innovation, cultural overhaul, and process evolution, all of which help organizations adapt to changing market environments.[13]

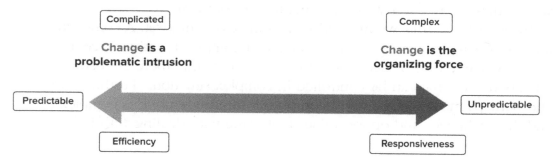

Embracing Complexity

> Once you recognize the realities of the complex world, there is no going back.
>
> *Jean G. Boulton et al., Embracing Complexity: Strategic*
> *Perspectives for an Age of Turbulence*

If we identify a problem we are trying to solve as a CAS, we need to accept the properties of a CAS rather than fight them. Applying CAS concepts suggests that a different approach should be taken to designing processes and managing projects, where we give up more control to the edges of the system, facilitate self-organization, accept sub-optimization, and tolerate a degree of chaos where we let things play out instead of trying to control them.

Applying the lessons of CAS can also help us build tools that are more robust, more innovative, self-organizing, and that can quickly adapt to changes in the environment.

Adopting a Complexity Mindset

> A complexity mindset recognizes that complexity creates both challenges and opportunities. It also creates an avenue for competitive advantage. If for no other reason, this should be more than enough motivation to develop a complexity mindset
>
> *Rick Nason, It's not complicated: The Art and Science*
> *of Complexity in Business*

If we identify a problem we are trying to solve as a CAS, we need to accept the properties of a CAS rather than fight them. Applying CAS concepts suggests that a different approach should be taken to managing work, where we give up more control to the edges of the system, facilitate self-organization, accept sub-optimization, and tolerate a degree of chaos where we let things play out instead of trying to control them.

In order to do this, we must adopt a complexity mindset. A complexity mindset is simply a mindset that accepts that complexity exists, accepts that complexity needs to be accounted for, and accepts that there are certain limitations on what can be controlled in complex situations. Furthermore, and perhaps most importantly, a complexity mindset embraces complexity and the challenges and opportunities that come with dealing with it.[14]

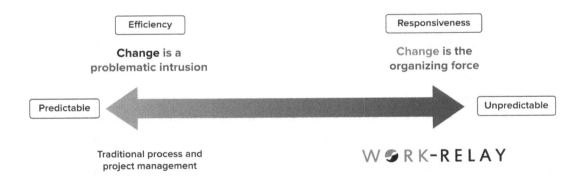

Accept That the Edge of Chaos is the Most Productive State

> Complexity should not be viewed as a burden to be avoided; we see it as a catalyst and an accelerator to create innovation and new ways of delivering value.
>
> *Juan Ramon Alaix, President, Pfizer*

Complexity calls for a different set of managerial assumptions and the recognition of how random events interact with ongoing local interactions to generate locally emergent effects and potentially significant system-level outcomes (e.g. a complexity perspective toward pm would focus on evaluating and responding to evolving conditions throughout the project rather than focusing on complying with a predetermined schedule).

It places much more value on acquiring and using current and particularized information for interim decisions. Consequently, employees must be made capable and competent to assume more responsibility and make appropriate decisions at the local level, rather than relying on a formal chain of command.

The edge of chaos is where the system is stable enough to remain viable but flexible enough to react quickly to changes in the environment There is sufficient freedom to keep the system vibrant, but enough stability to prevent a collapse into anarchy.

So while the term itself suggests that something has gone wrong, operating at the edge of chaos is actually healthy; scientists have shown that all large and complex systems tend to adapt this way. Whether in nature, society, economics, – or work management – systems must find the right balance between order and flexibility. This is because their survival and success depend on being able to constantly sense and adapt to changes in the environment they operate within.[15]

In a business context, operating at the edge of chaos opens up avenues for disruptive innovation, cultural overhaul, and process evolution, all of which help organizations adapt to changing market environments.

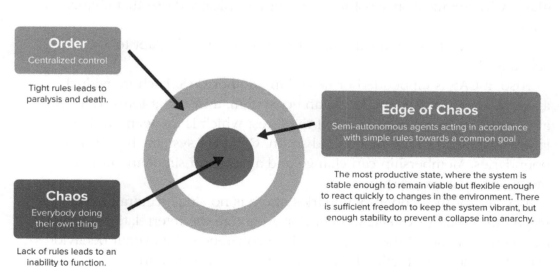

Accept Complexity

Accept that while complicated work can be automated, complex work cannot. Most work management endeavors of substance typically involve aspects that are complicated as well as complex. Being able to address both in the same solution is what we need.

Do not apply a complicated solution to a complex problem. It is likely to fail. That's why complex projects that involve instability face constant re-scheduling and difficulty accommodating change.

Complexity implies that there is a level of control available; but it is not complete control, and the situation is not completely manageable. This mode of management can be quite stressful if the manager has a complicated mindset that abhors ambiguity and uncertainty.

Accept Uncertainty

Sensitivity to initial conditions. No project is going to play out the same way every time.

This porous nature of CAS has severe implications for managing the system and is the primary reason for uncertainty and unpredictability. All systems exist within their own environment, and they are also part of that environment. Therefore, as the environment changes, they need to co-evolve – change to ensure a best fit. But because they are part of their environment, when they change they change their environment, and as it changes they need to change again; and so it goes on as a constant process (that's why the most successful systems are ironically those that change most often).

So, you need to build solutions that recognize and adapt to constant flux.

Also, a CAS is embedded or nested in another CAS. Each individual agent in a CAS is itself a CAS. In an ecosystem, a tree in a forest is a CAS and is also an agent in the CAS of the forest which is an agent in the larger ecosystem of the island, and so on. Complex systems have fuzzy boundaries. Membership can change and agents can simultaneously be members of several systems.

Because of these open boundaries, there is no single centralized control mechanism that governs CAS behavior. Although the interrelationships between elements of the system produce coherence, the overall behavior usually cannot be explained merely as the sum of each part.

Allow Solutions to Emerge

Allow the work plan to emerge rather than trying to force a rigid plan up front. This would suggest that you use the CAS concept of "chunking". You allow the work to emerge out of the links among simple systems that work well and are capable of operating independently. Allow the exact order and timing of events to emerge. The exact order and timing of events is not preordained before the work begins – it emerges from the interaction of the independent participants through an iterative learning process. Because a CAS can quickly learn and adapt and is capable of efficiently aggregating the collective intelligence of its many participants, it is a far better organizational model for knowledge workers.[16]

Find a workable decision; don't try to find the "best" decision. Start with something workable, then refine the decision by listening to reality and adapting constantly as new information and understanding arise. Therefore, when we plan we need to consider how planning can simplify execution and management, thereby reducing complexity.

Don't plan everything in detail, especially when working within an unpredictable and constantly changing environment. Complex situations do not lend themselves to a predetermined solution and it is folly to spend the time and energy even to attempt to. In projects, trying to schedule tasks in detail is a waste of effort.

Use minimal viable specifications. CAS suggests that the best way to plan is by establishing minimum specifications (what coarse-grained steps need to be done?), a general sense of direction (what is the ultimate objective?), and a few basic principles (e.g., how hand-offs take place) on how to get there. Once the minimum specifications have been set, individuals self-organize and adapt as time goes by to a continually changing context.[17]

Facilitate Self-organization

Think broad guidelines instead of specific instructions. Self-organization is a property of CAS, meaning that the system is capable of figuring out on its own how things should be done. In this sense the purpose of process/project design is not to provide specific rules for handling different situations, but to provide boundaries which ensure that the self-organizing processes (unhindered by unnecessary structure) are aimed in the right direction.

Allow teams to self-organize within the boundaries of discrete packages of work. A CAS is inherently self-organizing. Order, creativity, and progress can emerge naturally from the interactions within a CAS; it does not need to be imposed from outside. Creating the context for self-organization in work management means providing the tools needed to self-organize. The need for self-organization also makes participants more alert to changes and problems.

Distribute control so that decisions can be made as quickly and as closely to customers as possible.

Simplify!

Reduce the number of variables. Since everything affects everything else in a CAS, the more you have going on, the more chance you have of encountering complexity. Therefore, reduce the amount of work-in-progress (WIP) by limiting the amount of work in production, even if it means keeping some resources idle. This obviously reduces the amount of management that needs to take place at one time.

Focus, focus, focus! Complexity theory does not embrace the holism of Systems Theory (i.e. the notion that everything matters and everything has to be taken into account). Therefore, it is enough to find the elements of the system that really matter and focus on those.

Focus on leverage points. If you can, find a leverage point where you can make a small change and have a big impact. Find the constraints (bottlenecks) in the organization and focus on them. Just a few resources are critical in a project – typically less than 5 percent. Worry about their schedule – the others are likely to have enough capacity since they are not constrained. The project manager's job is not to keep everyone busy.

Focus on critical tasks. The same is true for tasks. Only a small percentage, maybe 20 percent of tasks in a project, is critical. Any task on the critical path is by definition critical, because if it is delayed the project completion will be delayed.

Focus and finish. Focusing on finishing instead of multi-tasking reduces complexity in scheduling, reduces multi-tasking, reduces wait times, etc. Concentrating resources on fewer projects at a time not only allows them to be executed faster, but it also reveals the overall capacity to undertake more projects.[18]

The role of a grand designer should be avoided in favor of the role of facilitation, orchestration, and creating enabling environments. Probably the most significant incentive for engaging in complicated thinking is the fear of non-control and its effect on our egos and sense of self-worth. But a project is a living system. Instead of trying to eliminate uncertainty and ambiguity in order to control the project, it's better to embrace uncertainty and better understand the dynamic found in the natural world of constantly evolving systems. A complexity perspective toward project management would focus on evaluating and responding to the evolving conditions throughout the project rather than focusing on complying with a predetermined schedule.

For a system to be resilient it must be capable of dynamic reorganization on the fly. That means that it must be capable of rapid coupling and decoupling while maintaining a degree of system coherence. Dynamic reorganization is greatly facilitated by modularity. This means small units that can combine and recombine, or even split off and reform with ease. Not so small that there is no coherence, but small enough for recombination.[19]

The greater the variety within the system the stronger it is. The ability to offer a broad range of responses to every situation encountered is critical for handling complexity.

CAS in Action

> And when it comes to solutions, simple is better. Elegant is better still. Elegance is the simplicity found on the far side of complexity.
> *Matthew May, The Elegant Solution: Toyota's Formula for Mastering Innovation*

The CAS mindset allows us to think more innovatively about solutions in general. Adopting a different frame of reference changes one's perspective so that what was remote and unnatural becomes sensible and natural.

The following examples provide a good general understanding of how looking at the world as a CAS can result in enormous benefits, typically with much less effort than a complicated solution would require.

Uber

Uber is a perfect example of an organization that took the complexity of their industry and turned its complexity into simplicity.

Uber provides us with a simple example of CAS properties in action – self-managing participants, following a set of simple rules, organize themselves to solve incredibly complex problems.

Uber is the master of work management.

Simple rules. Uber based their entire implementation on simple rules:

- Drivers can work whenever they want.
- Uber takes 20 percent of all fares.
- Riders pay automatically through their registered credit card.
- Riders can rate drivers and vice versa.

Note that the rules are not only simple, they are also unchangeable. That's what keeps them simple.

Attractors. The cost of a ride, and therefore payment to the driver, increases when it rains, thereby encouraging more drivers to be available to meet the inevitable increase in demand. In addition, surge pricing is used as an incentive to get more drivers to a specific area.

Emergence. Drivers will learn to congregate around areas that are most likely to give them the most pick-ups.

Synchronization. Drivers synchronize their routes to ensure there is not too much overlap, which would reduce the chance of them getting a call.

Feedback. Quality is self-managing through ratings. Drivers with better ratings are given precedence over those with lower ratings. Drivers rating passengers ensures good behavior on the part of the passenger, who could lose the use of the service if their rating gets too low.

Requisite variety. There are multiple types of rides available, like UberX and Black Car services.

Self-organization. Self-organization is prevalent throughout the system, from drivers keeping their own schedules and deciding where to go, to being responsible for the state of their vehicle.

Sub-optimality. Cars may not be available in certain areas at certain times. It's an accepted part of the system.

Chunking. Uber treats its drivers as modules that can be used in different ways. For example, they can deliver food with Uber Eats. They could be used to deliver Amazon packages. The drivers and their vehicles are simply autonomous entities that can be used in different ways by providing a different framework – like Lego blocks.

Cemex

This example illustrates the attempt to apply a complicated solution to a complex problem vs. the utilization of a complexity mindset to solve a complex problem.

The Problem

The problem for Cemex, a global building materials company, was how to improve the delivery of wet cement to construction sites at the precise point in time that it is needed.

These deliveries never proceed on schedule because construction sites' state of readiness is dependent on so many unpredictable elements, resulting in ever-changing schedules of building sites. The difficulties in timing are compounded by traffic delays, poor roads, a truck breaking down, lost paperwork, bad weather, etc.

The result is that sites are often ready earlier than planned (high-cost workers then hang around awaiting the delivery with nothing to do), or are not ready as planned (the cement then starts to harden in the truck).

To avoid uncertainty, customers placed multiple orders, hoping one would showed up at the right time and cancelling others when they did not, causing further chaos for Cemex.

The Complicated Solution

Cemex tried to enforce rigid advance reservations through centralized organization, which, when things went wrong (as they always did), only made matters worse ("Sorry, we can't reschedule you until next week").

The Result

An on-time delivery rate of less than 35 percent, and lots of unhappy customers.

The Complex Solution

Cemex implemented a self-organizing distributed intelligence model. Instead of rigidly trying to schedule everything ahead of time in an environment of chaos, Cemex lets the drivers themselves schedule deliveries ad hoc and in real time. The drivers form a flock of trucks criss-crossing the town. If a contractor calls in an order, the available truck closest to the site at that time makes the delivery. Dispatchers ensure customer creditworthiness and guard against omissions, but the agents in the field have permission and the information they need to schedule orders on the fly.

How It Works

Cemex loads its fleets of cement trucks each morning and dispatches them with no preordained destination.

The trick lies in how they make their rounds. Like ants scavenging a territory, they are guided to their destination by simple rules.

- Rule #1: Deliver as much cement as rapidly as possible to as many costumers as possible.
- Rule #2: Avoid duplication of effort by staying as far away from other cement trucks as possible.

Cemex provided GPS real-time location signals from every truck, massive telecommunications throughout the company, and full information available to drivers and dispatchers, with the authority to act on it.

The result:

An on-time delivery rate of 98 percent, with just a two-hour window, and a promise of a 20 percent discount if your delivery is late, as well as less wastage of hardened cement and much happier customers.

The Magic Roundabout

The Problem

The intersection includes traffic from a football stadium, it sits right next to a fire station, and combines those facilities with five other major roads.

The Goal

Enable the continuous movement of traffic despite unpredictable situations.
Key parameters:

- extreme variable traffic;
- the need to allow locals to get to where they need to go quickly;

- protect those unfamiliar with the nature of such a roundabout from causing traffic jams and accidents;
- overall ensure a very low incidence of traffic accidents.

The Complicated Approach

- Gather traffic engineering specialists;
- Look at the most advanced traffic light systems with proven algorithms for traffic management.

The result:

- Traffic build-up for miles because the system is not able to anticipate and account for the high variability in traffic patterns.
- Higher incidence of accidents because people are paying more attention to the rules of the stop lights than the cars around them.

The CAS Approach

Create a lightly constrained system in which agent (driver) decisions can change very quickly based on circumstances (the system) – decisions about how to interpret the traffic flows, when to go and when to stop, which way to turn, and so on are offloaded to drivers.
The result:

- No central authority is needed or desired.
- No traffic lights.
- Continuously flowing traffic.
- Since it was introduced it has never jammed up.
- Significantly fewer collisions occur and they are typically minor and cause few injuries since they occur at low speeds.

Conclusion

This is an excellent example of attractors and barriers creating desired behavior with a light hand:

- Roundabouts are designed to promote a continuous, circular flow of traffic. Because traffic is constantly flowing through the intersection, drivers don't have the incentive to speed up to try and "beat the light" like they might at a traditional intersection.

■ Roads entering a roundabout are gently curved to direct drivers into the intersection and help them travel counter-clockwise around the roundabout. The curved roads and one-way travel around the roundabout eliminate the possibility for T-bone and head-on collisions.[20]

Notes

1. Agile Project Management – CC Pace. www.ccpace.com/asset_files/ AgileProjectManagement.pdf.
2. A Complexity Science Primer: What is Complexity Science. https:// perfectcustompapers.com/a-complexity-science-primer-what-is-complexity-science-and-why-should-i-learn-about-it-adapted-from-edgeware-lessons-from-complexity-science-for-health-care-leaders-by-brenda-zimmerman-curt-lind/.
3. Complexity Theory Basic Concepts – SlideShare. www.slideshare.net/ johncleveland/complexity-theory-basic-concepts.
4. Peter Fryer, A Brief Description of Complex Adaptive. https://integral-options.blogspot.com/2013/03/peter-fryer-brief-description-of.html.
5. Rod Collins, The Management Wisdom of Complex Adaptive Systems. https://optimityadvisors.com/insights/blog/ management-wisdom-complex-adaptive-systems.
6. Complex Adaptive Systems | Beyond Intractability. www. beyondintractability.org/essay/complex_adaptive_systems.
7. Complex Systems and the Darnall-Preston Complexity Index. https:// saylordotorg.github.io/text_project-management-from-simple-to-complex-v1.1/s04-03-complex-systems-and-the-darnal.html.
8. Edge.org. www.edge.org/response-detail/27150.
9. Edge.org. www.edge.org/response-detail/27150.
10. A Complexity Science Primer: What is Complexity Science. https:// perfectcustompapers.com/a-complexity-science-primer-what-is-complexity-science-and-why-should-i-learn-about-it-adapted-from-edgeware-lessons-from-complexity-science-for-health-care-leaders-by-brenda-zimmerman-curt-lind/.
11. A Complexity Science Primer: What is Complexity Science. https:// perfectcustompapers.com/a-complexity-science-primer-what-is-complexity-science-and-why-should-i-learn-about-it-adapted-from-edgeware-lessons-from-complexity-science-for-health-care-leaders-by-brenda-zimmerman-curt-lind/.

12. A Complexity Science Primer: What is Complexity Science. https://perfectcustompapers.com/a-complexity-science-primer-what-is-complexity-science-and-why-should-i-learn-about-it-adapted-from-edgeware-lessons-from-complexity-science-for-health-care-leaders-by-brenda-zimmerman-curt-lind/.

13. Order from Chaos: How to Apply Complexity Theory at Work. www.bbva.com/en/order-from-chaos-how-to-apply-complexity-theory-at-work/.

14. The Critical Difference between Complex and Complicated. https://sloanreview.mit.edu/article/the-critical-difference-between-complex-and-complicated/.

15. Order from Chaos: How to Apply Complexity Theory at Work. www.bbva.com/en/order-from-chaos-how-to-apply-complexity-theory-at-work/.

16. The Real-world Basis for Situational Process Management. www.work-relay.com/blog/the-real-world-basis-for-situational-process/.

17. Working Paper: Some Emerging Principles for Managers of Complex Adaptive Systems (CAS) by Paul E. Plsek. www.directedcreativity.com/pages/ComplexityWP.html.

18. Improving Focus, Predictability, and Team Morale on Projects. www.slideshare.net/JosephCooperPMP/pmi-congress-ccpm-final.

19. Seven Characteristics of Resilience – Cognitive Edge. http://cognitive-edge.com/blog/seven-characteristics-of-resilience/.

20. Roundabout Benefits | WSDOT. www.wsdot.wa.gov/Safety/roundabouts/benefits.htm.

Chapter 4

A Sense-making Framework for Project Management

It is of course not as simple as changing one's perspective from seeing project management as a complicated endeavor to one that is seen as a complex problem to be solved.

In fact, most projects consist of elements that are simple, complicated, complex, and chaotic. The key is to know which part of the project fits into each category, and approach them in the manner appropriate to the challenges they pose.

Cynefin

A Welsh academic/consultant named Dave Snowden created a model called *Cynefin* (pronounced "kenevin") to provide a generic description of the world and how we deal with it. It applies to systems (in the broadest sense), situations, and our responses. It is also very applicable to processes and projects.

In simplest terms, the Cynefin framework exists to help us realize that all situations are not created equal and to help us understand that different situations require different responses to successfully navigate them.[1]

In most projects there are likely to be parts of the project that fit into each domain. Therefore,

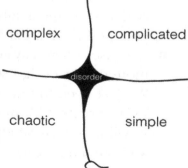

to implement the best solution, it is critical to understand which parts of the project fit into each domain.

The Domains

> Depending on which space you're in you should think differently rather than the one size fits all that has been the tradition of management theory.
>
> *Dave Snowden*

The Simple Domain

The simple domain is characterized by the following attributes:

- There are known cause-and-effect relationships, and these relationships are repeatable, perceivable, predictable, and can be determined in advance.
- Activities can usually be codified and documented into standard operating procedures and work instructions, and may even be automated.
- Best suited for command-and control style of management.

The Complicated Domain

The complicated ("knowable") domain is characterized by the following attributes:

- The links between cause and effect are less apparent and not self-evident but are able to be uncovered.
- Complicated activities are predictable and repeatable. They require blueprints, detailed organizational mechanisms, and checklists.
- You determine what possible practices would be appropriate for dealing with the situation and then, having selected one (based, perhaps, on the availability of experts in that particular domain), you then implement and execute this practice.[2]
- Because ordered systems display predictable outcomes, we can more or less design solutions that have a good chance of working. We just need to understand the system well enough and enlist the right experts if it's unclear what to do. Once we have a solution, it will be transferable from one context to another (e.g. designing and building a car).

The Complex Domain

The complex ("unknowable") domain is characterized by the following attributes:

- The links between cause and effect are only clear in retrospect.
- Activities function in a fluid, unpredictable environment.
- You cannot control events – there are too many interacting variables – so you can only influence the environment.
- To do this requires a set of simple principles that guide and shape the system.
- These simple principles are established through trial and error, using attractors and boundaries and seeing what happens. An attractor is something that draws the system toward it. A boundary is something that contains the work.
- Once you have found a solution that works you continue to monitor it, adjust it as necessary, and extract the heuristics of how it works.[3]
- Heuristics are experience-based, operating principles that can be observed and applied across contexts.
- When a heuristic has a good result, we amplify it. When it has a poor result, we dampen it. Strategies for amplification and dampening depend on the context and the problem.
- Energies must concentrate on flexibility, highlighting the importance of keeping one's options open (a world of "safe" mistakes). In such a scenario, the basic hypothesis is that the future is unpredictable rather than predictable.

The Chaotic Domain

The chaotic ("unknowable") domain is characterized by the following attributes:

- There are no cause-and-effect relationships.
- There is no point looking for the right answers (as no right answer exists).
- The first thing that needs to be done is to take some action (which may or may not work) in an attempt to stabilize the environment and reduce the chaotic nature of the project.

Disorder

The disorder domain in the center represents situations where there is no clarity about which of the other domains apply. By definition, it is hard to see when this domain applies. According to Snowden, the way out of this realm is to break down the situation into constituent parts and assign each to one of the other four realms. Leaders can then make decisions and intervene in contextually appropriate ways.[4]

Domain Properties

The Role of Constraints for Each Domain

Constraints

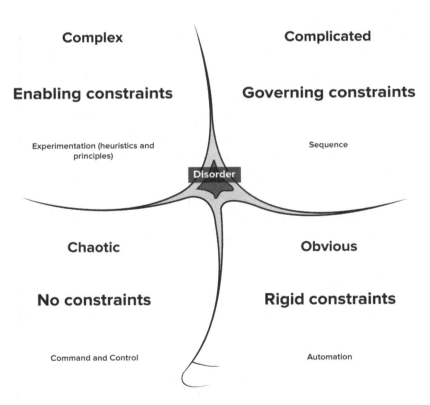

■ **The complicated domain** requires governing constraints – a set of rules ensures that things are always done in exactly the same way every time. Rules set limits to action; they contain all possible instances of action.

- **The complex domain** requires enabling constraints – you have the latitude to do whatever you think makes sense at the time provided a specified set of rules aren't broken. They provide measurable guidance which can adapt to the unknowable unknowns.

The Role of Cause and Effect for Each Domain

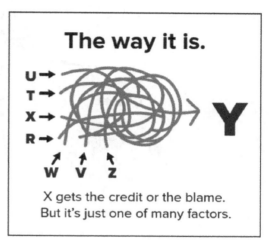

The way it looks.

X → Y

Linear, Predictable

Focused on the end result

X gets the credit or the blame.

The way it is.

X gets the credit or the blame.
But it's just one of many factors.

Managers THINK they understand the relationships between cause and effect in their organizations. But in fact, the links between actions and results are infinitely more complicated than most managers suspect. As a result, managers are prisoners of the very systems they are supposed to manage. They understand neither the underlying dynamics of these systems nor how to influence those dynamics to achieve organizational goals.

Indeed, the idea of the manager as an omniscient scientific planner is fundamentally misguided. According to Senge, "The perception that someone 'up there' is in control is based on an illusion – the illusion that anyone could master the dynamic and detailed complexity of an organization from the top."

– David H. Freedman, *Is Management Still a Science?* (Harvard Business Review)

Our entire education is confined to the simple and the complicated domains. That is after all how school is designed – the teacher looks for the right answer and there always is a right answer in that framework. At work, we have also mainly lived in stable environments where there was a lot of predictability and where doing better was a process of optimization of known rules and known outcomes. We could use engineering precepts to plan. Above all we sought to find the right answer and we tested it against the knowns of cause and effect.

Cause and Effect

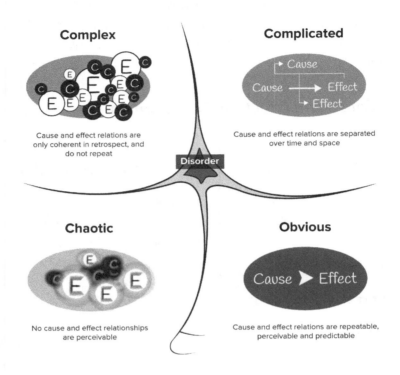

Complex

Cause and effect relations are only coherent in retrospect, and do not repeat

Complicated

Cause and effect relations are separated over time and space

Disorder

Chaotic

No cause and effect relationships are perceivable

Obvious

Cause and effect relations are repeatable, perceivable and predictable

Domain Shift

With the increase in knowledge, there is a "clockwise shift" from chaotic through complex and complicated to simple. Similarly, a build-up of biases complacency, or lack of maintenance can cause a "catastrophic failure": a clockwise movement from simple to chaotic. There can be counter-clockwise movement as people die and knowledge is forgotten, or as new generations question the rules; and a counter-clockwise push from chaotic to simple can occur when a lack of order causes rules to be imposed suddenly.[5]

Cynefin for Project Management

Applying Cynefin to project management helps us understand which aspects of project management fall into each domain, so that the appropriate action can be taken that will yield the best results.

See the following examples.

Project Management

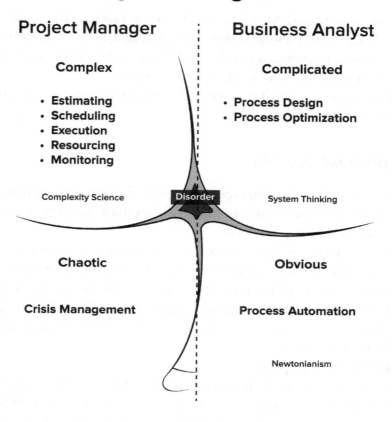

Project Manager	**Business Analyst**
Complex	**Complicated**
• **Estimating** • **Scheduling** • **Execution** • **Resourcing** • **Monitoring**	• **Process Design** • **Process Optimization**
Complexity Science	System Thinking
Disorder	
Chaotic	**Obvious**
Crisis Management	**Process Automation**
	Newtonianism

Skills

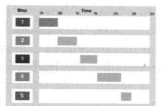

Manage by Project

I use the process design to manage the project

- Schedules tasks
- Track dates against schedule
- Report task and project status
- Assign resources
- Monitor time, cost, quality
- Take care of deviations
- Resolve issues

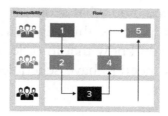

Design by Process

I design the process:

- the tasks that need to be done
- the sequence of tasks
- the skills needed for tasks
- the responsibility for the tasks
- the estimated duration of tasks
- the data to be collected by tasks
- the rules that govern work transition

The Simple Domain

There may be certain activities that need to take place in the same way, every time. These may include things like getting approvals at certain points during the project, updating a database at the conclusion of some task, ensuring compliance but checking business rules.

Many of these things can be automated given the appropriate project management platform.

The Complicated Domain

In the context of project management, projects that operate in this space would be ones where the domain of execution is known, regular, predictable, and with very low risk.

Traditional project management considers a project as a simple structure in a stable environment with a predictable future. Success under this condition ensues from balance and stability. Orientation to stability highlights balance, and therefore assigning all resources to the maintenance of a predictable situation (a world safe from mistakes) becomes especially important in such a scenario.

This is the domain of process.

There is an unfortunate delineation in the software market that places "processes" and "projects" into different categories of software. This makes no sense, because projects clearly have processes that they depend on, and processes obviously have a timeline.

All repetitive projects contain well-understood processes – a series of activities that must take place in sequence, or in parallel, or based on contingencies. Unlike activities in the simple domain, there is no single way to get things done – there may be variations based on circumstances and human decision making. But the process is generally understood and can be easily followed most of the time. Exceptions may arise, but there are usually procedures in place to handle them.

Design is complicated. Design is primarily about mapping out what tasks need to be done, and what sequence they need to be done in. Especially for process-driven projects, this will be relatively stable throughout the project. For example, you know that in order for the installation of equipment to take place you need to have scheduled the installer, the hardware needs to have arrived, etc.

The Complex Domain

Once we start adding dates to the plan, we move into the realm of complexity. Scheduling, status tracking, and resource management are all complex problems. There is no way to predict with any certainty how things are going to play out. Regardless of that, the tasks that need to be done and their sequence remains relatively intact inside a module (e.g. you always have to ship the equipment before you can install it), while the combination of modules may be different.

A project plan is constantly in flux – *not* the project design.

Managing shared resources is an obvious aspect of project management that falls into the complex domain. There is no clearly defined way to do this because there are way too many variables – project dates change, people leave or get sick, different skills are required – the list goes on and on.

So instead of trying to create a complicated solution – a resourcing schedule to be adhered to – it is better to specify some key principles and use those principles to guide the way to emergent solutions.

Other implications of applying CAS to projects are as follows.

Emergence. Focus on evaluating and responding to the evolving conditions throughout the project rather than focusing on complying with a predetermined schedule.

Sub-optimality. Grand design should be avoided in favor of the role of facilitation, orchestration, and creating enabling environments. Since dates always change, there is no point in spending time trying to predict dates and then trying to maintain them as the deadlines go whooshing by. In project management, creating a schedule to keep equilibrium will make it fragile and subject to bad consequences

Distributed control. Control should be dispersed throughout the project. A CAS is inherently self-organizing. Order, creativity, and progress can emerge naturally from the interactions within a CAS; it does not need to be imposed from outside. Allow teams to self-organize within the boundaries of discrete packages of work.

Nested systems. In project management, for example, a project is impacted not just by what happens inside the project. The project itself is part of a portfolio of projects, which in turn is part of the organization, and the organization is impacted by its market and relationships. The borders are fuzzy, and each level of the system can impact all others.

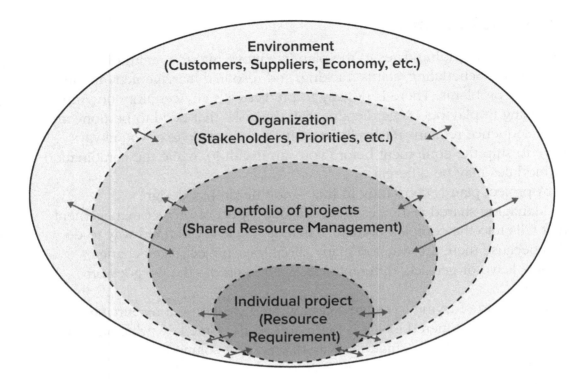

There are complex relationships at play between the stakeholders –
people as well as sub-systems that make up the project. Not just that; inside
each sub-system that has a stake there are interrelationships that affect how
that sub-system reacts and responds to certain situations and players. The
system behavior is governed by all of these interrelationships and is clearly
distributed control. No one player truly calls the shots.

Focus and finish. Focusing on finishing instead of multi-tasking reduces
complexity in scheduling, reduces multi-tasking, reduces wait times, etc.
Concentrating resources on fewer projects at a time not only allows them to
be executed faster, but it also reveals the overall capacity to undertake more
projects.

Reduce complexity. There are ways to reduce the number of variables
that have to be dealt with:

■ Reduce the amount of work-in-progress (WIP). Limit the number of projects
in execution, even if it means keeping some resources idle. This obviously
reduces the amount of management that needs to take place at one time.

■ Focus on leverage points. If you can, find a leverage point where
you can make a small change and have a big impact. Find the

constraints in the organization and focus on them. Just a few resources are critical in a project – typically less than 5 percent. Worry about their schedule – the others are likely to have enough capacity, since they are not constrained. The project manager's job is not to keep everyone busy.

The Chaotic Domain

The chaotic domain is one that a project manager always hopes to stay out of. You enter the chaotic domain when something happens that is completely out of the ordinary and has an immediate impact on the course of the project, and must therefore be dealt with immediately.

Examples include a dramatic change in resource availability, a significant change in the requirements, a cataclysmic event of some kind (what insurance companies call an "Act of God"), etc.

A Difference in Skill Sets

The skills required to address the ordered domains (simple and complicated) are very different from those required to handle the unordered (complex and chaotic) domains.

In the same way that you wouldn't want a business analyst to be the one to resolve a chaotic situation, you wouldn't want a project manager to get into the weeds of how the business works.

A project manager does not have the same set of skills as a business process analyst and vice versa. Having a project manager doing business analysis, or a business analyst doing project management – what could go wrong?

Summary

The key is having the wisdom to know which system is appropriate and the courage to apply the proper techniques for that system are the first and perhaps the most effective steps to gaining competitive advantage with complexity.

Rick Nason

Complex situations do not lend themselves to a solution, and it is folly to spend the time, energy, or effort even to attempt to create solutions. Yet this is exactly how the complicated way of thinking works. It is in evidence when companies try to optimize complex activities like project management.

Taking the time to make an accurate judgment about the type of management problem at hand helps avoid the arrogance of complicated thinking. Complicated thinking leads managers to think that they are doing something purposeful when in reality they are not, and in fact they are likely doing more harm than good.[6]

Notes

1. Julia Wester, Understanding the Cynefin Framework – A Basic Introduction. www.everydaykanban.com/2013/09/29/understanding-the-cynefin-framework/.
2. Figuring Out Your Project's Landscape Using the Cynefin. http://quantmleap.com/blog/2014/03/figuring-out-your-projects-landscape-using-the-cynefin-framework/.
3. Explaining Cynefin for Strategy and Decision Making. www.chriscorrigan.com/parkinglot/explaining-cynefin-for-strategy-and-decision-making/.
4. Cynefin Framework – Wikipedia. https://en.wikipedia.org/wiki/Cynefin_Framework.
5. Cynefin Framework – Wikipedia. https://en.wikipedia.org/wiki/Cynefin_Framework.
6. The Critical Difference between Complex and Complicated. https://sloanreview.mit.edu/article/the-critical-difference-between-complex-and-complicated/.

Chapter 5

The DNA of Projects

How Do We Create a Work Environment that Can Effectively Absorb Complexity?

> Simplicity is a great virtue but it requires hard work to achieve it and education to appreciate it. And to make matters worse: complexity sells better.
>
> *Edsger Dijkstra[1]*

A Single Work Management Platform

If in fact projects beyond the most simple include work that falls into Snowden's four categories, it becomes obvious that the tendency to split the management of work up into different applications makes no sense. Since project work can fit into any of the categories, we need a unified, comprehensive system in which they can be managed.

This is a problem, because if you were to go to an imaginary software application supermarket there is an aisle for project management software, and an aisle for process management software. There is no aisle for process/project management software.

A single, comprehensive, unified platform for defining, visualizing, and driving the flow of project work through the organization has a number of benefits:

- One tool implementation and support for both processes and projects.
- The same interface for users involved in processes and projects.

- An added dimension of time for processes.
- An added dimension of process management for projects.
- Responsibilities for process design and project management can be assumed by resources with the appropriate skill set.
- No importing and exporting between multiple tools, or duplication of data. No duplication of effort designing in one tool and managing in another.
- A singe repository for all the organization's processes and projects.

A tool that is capable of providing both project and process management will yield enormous dividends.

The DNA of Work

We could have had thousands of elements in the periodic table. DNA could have had millions of different bases. We could have designed computers to store files with 0s, 1s and 2s.

But that's not what happened. The best-designed, most elegant systems are simple yet powerful. Simplicity gives them reliability, and a clever arrangement of parts gives them power.

Other examples of this include the following:

- An infinite array of colors can be constructed from just four: cyan (a shade of blue), magenta, yellow, and black – what printers and designers call "CMYK".
- Simple self-locking building bricks (Lego) provide for a vast variety of combinations of the bricks for making structures of many different kinds and shapes.

By the same token, a work management platform also comprises a small number of elements that can be combined and recombined in myriad different ways to match the prevailing circumstances.

It doesn't matter whether that work is part of a task management, process management, or project management system. It's still just work.

Because, after all, what is work?

The definition of work is *"an activity involving mental or physical effort done in order to achieve a purpose or result"*.

"Work" is basically about turning intent into reality. If you are given a task like "Write a report", it may be a stand-alone task. Or it may be a step in a larger sequence of steps (a process). Or it may be a task in a Gantt chart as part of a project. It doesn't matter – it's still just work. Why not treat it that way?

Why adopt all these different approaches to work task management, project management, process management, case management, etc. when the underlying elements are simple and can be combined in any number of ways?

Work essentially comprises three primary elements:

1. **A unit of work.** What needs to be done, how long should it take, and what skills are needed to accomplish it?
2. **The flow of work.** What sequence does the work follow?
3. **The timeline of work.** When does the work need to be completed?

Let's investigate these elements in more detail.

A Unit of Work

A unit of work can be a stand-alone task, a step in a process, an activity in a case, or a task in a project.

- The name is expressed as a verb and the name reflects its result or output (e.g. *Create a Report, Send an invoice*).
- It delivers a result that is unique and unambiguous.
- A single person is responsible for getting the work completed.
- It includes an estimated duration.
- It may include any number of other properties, including the following.

The Flow of Work

Any work that involves more than one person has a flow. This flow of work is organized in a process.

- A process is an operationally independent series of steps.
- Since they exist independently of each other, processes can be maintained independently.
- Processes can be assembled in any combination, like a set of Lego blocks.
- Any process can be a parent or child process in a hierarchy of processes.
- The process has an estimated duration. This is the sum of the longest series of step durations in the process.
- Processes are triggered by an event (e.g. manual execution, the completion of a previous process, a database update, etc.).
- Process names reflect the deliverable of the process (e.g. *Packaging, Engineering*).
- The people assigned to the steps in a process are collectively responsible as a team for the successful completion of the process.
- Processes support the full spectrum of structure, from fully structured to ad hoc, as well as providing the ability to mix and match process types as needed.

The Timeline of Work

When the timeline of a process needs to be managed (i.e. there are deadlines that must be met), the process becomes a project.

- A project can consist of one or more related processes.
- Individual units of work have an expected and an actual duration.
- They can be given start and end dates.
- The timeline of work is typically shown in a Gantt chart.

Name	Duration	Start Date Planned	Completed Date Planned	Responsibility
⊟ Creative	49d			Project Manager
⊟ S-Creative	49d			
Copy Development	4d	08-Sep-2014	11-Sep-2014	Graphic Designer
Internal Review	1d	12-Sep-2014	12-Sep-2014	Design Manager
Revisions	1d	15-Sep-2014	15-Sep-2014	Graphic Designer
Layout Development	8d	16-Sep-2014	25-Sep-2014	Graphic Designer
Internal Review	1d	26-Sep-2014	26-Sep-2014	Design Manager
⊟ Pharmaceutical Project	158d			
Job Start Meeting	0d	20-Aug-2014	20-Aug-2014	Project Manager
⊟ Documentation	35d			Project Manager
⊟ S-Documentation	35d			
⊟ Business Requirements Document	19d			Analyst
⊟ S-BRD	19d			
Create BRD	13d	20-Aug-2014	05-Sep-2014	Analyst
Internal Review	1d	08-Sep-2014	08-Sep-2014	Analyst
Revisions	2d	09-Sep-2014	10-Sep-2014	Analyst
Client Review	2d	11-Sep-2014	12-Sep-2014	Analyst
Client Approval	1d	15-Sep-2014	15-Sep-2014	Analyst
⊟ Functional Requirements Document	7d			Analyst
⊟ S-FRD	7d			
Internal Review	1d	16-Sep-2014	16-Sep-2014	Technical Designer
Revisions	3d	17-Sep-2014	19-Sep-2014	Technical Designer
Client Review	2d	22-Sep-2014	23-Sep-2014	Technical Designer
Client Approval	1d	24-Sep-2014	24-Sep-2014	Technical Designer

That's it.

Everything you need to manage work comes down to these three elements.

Summary

In the real world, achieving a business objective typically requires work that is structured and unstructured, predictable and unpredictable, temporary and repetitive. Having disparate tools to manage these different types of work introduces an unnecessary level of complexity into the work environment.

The solution is to create a platform comprising a small number of work elements that can be combined and recombined in myriad different ways to match the prevailing circumstances.

Note

1. Edsger W. Dijkstra > Quotes > Quotable Quote – Goodreads. www. goodreads.com/quotes/215637-simplicity-is-a-great-virtue-but-it-requires-hard-work.

PROJECT MANAGEMENT AS A COMPLEX ADAPTIVE SYSTEM

If an organization needs the ability to not only survive but also thrive on fast-paced change, it needs to have the primary capabilities of sensing, adapting, and responding to the changing business environment. A machine by definition is lifeless and therefore does not have the capabilities to sense, adapt, and respond. Hence it is necessary to infuse life into organizations by modeling them using the principles of CAS, so that they can embrace change.[1]

Note

1. Q&A on the Book Enterprise Agility. infoq.com. www.infoq.com/articles/book-review-enterprise-agility.

Chapter 6

Design

How Do We Create a Project Environment that Can Effectively Absorb Complexity?

> Plans are worthless, but planning is everything. There is a
> very great distinction because when you are planning for an
> emergency you must start with this one thing: the very definition
> of "emergency" is that it is unexpected, therefore it is not going to
> happen the way you are planning.
>
> *Dwight D. Eisenhower*

One of the most difficult challenges companies face today is how to be more flexible, agile, and adaptive in a dynamic, volatile business environment. How do you build a company that can identify and capitalize on opportunities, navigate around risks and other challenges, and respond quickly to changes in the environment?[1]

For a system to do this, it must be capable of dynamic reorganization on the fly. That means it must be capable of rapid coupling and decoupling while maintaining a degree of system coherence.

Design is in the complicated domain. If you find the right subject matter expert, you should be able to find a way to design a process that provides the "right" way to get things done.

But it doesn't end there. While it is "complicated" to come up with a process, the execution of a process or series of processes is often complex. How the processes are strung together at run time may be different depending on different sometimes unforeseen circumstances. Therefore, the design phase of project management must account not only for the complicated sequences of tasks, it must also account for the sequence in which the processes are executed, which may be different every time.

For example, if you offered 100 different services, and each service was mapped out carefully in how to deliver that service, the client may choose a combination of services unique to their needs. In this case, the project plan may be dynamically constructed, based on decisions made during execution and dependencies among the processes behind the services.

It is therefore critical to account for the complex nature of execution in the design process.

(Note: Modularization is the opposite of reductionism. With reductionism you start with the whole, and then break down the whole into its constituent parts. With modularization you start with the parts, and the whole emerges and can only be seen in retrospect.)

Modularity

> The only way to make a complex system that works is to begin with a simple system that works. Complexity is created by assembling it incrementally from simple modules that can operate independently.
>
> *Kevin Kelly, Out of Control, the Rise of Neo-biological Civilization*

Complex systems emerge out of simple systems that work well. Modularity is ubiquitous in Complex Adaptive Systems. The CAS concept of "chunking" simply means that a good approach to building complex systems is to start small. Experiment to get pieces that work, and then link the pieces together. Complex systems emerge out of the links among simple systems that work well and are capable of operating independently, but interact with their environment as a single unit. They provide the most widespread means of complexity, in both natural and artificial systems.

Modules are small, simple, stand-alone processes designed to do one thing well. A module is a self-contained collection of functionality that delivers a predetermined result, like "Customer credit history verification", or "Contract approval". It is typically made up of multiple tasks performed by multiple people, usually in a predefined sequence, and can include any number of other modules. In work management, a module is a process.

Dynamic reorganization is greatly facilitated by modularity. This means small units that can combine and recombine, or even split off and reform with ease. Not so small that there is no coherence, but small enough for recombination. Processes are componentized as reusable services. So any

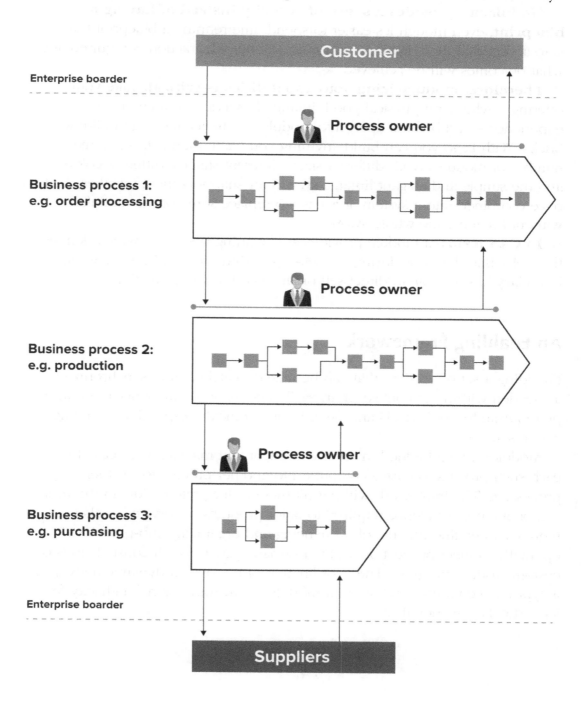

process can be a parent, child, or linked process. This allows the system to dynamically organize and reorganize processes on the fly, like Lego blocks. And once combined, it is easy to replace some of the modules without breaking the whole end-to-end process.

Modularity provides a sense of security instead of having a blueprint, even though it's easier to spend time refining a blueprint than it is to accept that there is much uncertainty about what action is required and what outcomes will be achieved.

Therefore, modularizing your capabilities is critical. Take your offering – whether a physical good, intangible service, or memorable experience – and break it apart into modular elements like Lego building bricks. With Lego you can build anything you want, thanks to the large number of modules (with different sizes, different shapes, different colors) and the simple and elegant linkage system for snapping them together. And once combined into a system, it is easy to replace some of the modules without breaking the whole system.

In CAS terms, a module provides a containing boundary which defines the "self" that develops during the self-organizing process. The containing boundary has the role to direct self-organization to value creation.

An Enabling Framework

Providing a set of services that can be mixed, matched, and synchronized as needed within the context of an easily understood framework is a critical prerequisite for individuals and organizations quickly respond to changing circumstances.

Modules are embedded in an environment that makes it very easy for each such process to pass its output on to another process for further processing. The framework will permit them to integrate rapidly in the best combination or sequence required to tailor products or services. It also requires an engine capable of sequencing and organizing sub-processes optimally to meet production and performance goals for all constellations of custom work-in-progress. The coordination of the overall dynamic network is typically centralized, while each module retains operational authority for its particular functionality.

Benefits of Modularization

- **Encourages team ownership.** The people assigned to tasks in a module are collectively responsible as a team for the successful completion of the module. Modules facilitate team ownership of team commitments instead of individual ownership of individual commitments. In a modular system, the burden of creativity and intelligence is on the people in the module. In a module, your focus is on solving problems and delivering value rather than executing previously defined steps. The module provides the "self" in self-organization.

- **Facilitates experimentation.** One of the key approaches to mastering complexity is experimentation. When modules are autonomous, they can try new things without worrying about a "ripple effect" that will disrupt the activities of other units. They can adopt new tools and practices quickly without having to ask permission.[2] They can be flexible in the ways that they choose to respond to customer requests. This means that each module can be free to innovate, try new things, adjust its work process, and so on. The flexibility this provides gives participants the ability to apply their knowledge and not simply follow rules.

- **Establishes a standard approach.** The ability to create a library of process fragments or sub-processes that can be linked together as required helps avoid inconsistencies, errors, and ambiguities, thus ensuring that the project plan follows process standards.

- **Facilitates versioning.** The ability to maintain multiple versions of a process. This provides enormous flexibility in maintaining processes and eliminating the need for duplication and manual changes to a project plan if modules change while in progress.

- **Distributes control.** Control is distributed so that decisions can be made as quickly and as closely to customers as possible.

- **Enables faster decision making.** One of the key goals of modular design is to reduce interdependency by enabling autonomous modules to focus on clear outcomes that deliver value to the project. This way, decisions can be made as quickly and as close to customers as possible. There is no way for people to respond and adapt quickly if they have to get permission before they can do anything.

- **Keeps options open.** With sufficient modularization, it is not necessary to specify in detail what needs to be done until the last responsible moment. This keeps your options open. Flexibility comes from delaying design decisions and the start of major activities for key project drivers (information flows, technical decisions, and business decisions) until the last responsible moment; that is, the latest moment possible without compromising cost or schedule. This "keep your options open" approach allows for maximum flexibility.
- **Provides auditability.** What were previously ad hoc tasks done outside the defined process become part of the process, providing visibility and auditability. There is no need for participants to step outside the system into the black hole of email and spreadsheets.
- **Providing a competitive edge.** Being able to make changes on the fly provides a competitive edge – you are taking the knowledge that is in workers' heads and applying it directly in business operations.
- **Facilitating innovation.** Processes become adaptable to changes in the environment in the normal course of business. The flexibility this provides gives participants the ability to apply their knowledge and not simply follow rules.
- **Eliminates the need for defining details of end-to-end processes.** There is no need to define, and get agreement on a complete end-to-end process, something that can take a significant amount of time and becomes difficult to modify if everyone involved has to reach agreement when changes are required.

Summary

The best way to build a complex system is to modularize it.

Complex systems emerge out of the links among simple systems that work well and can operate independently but interact with their environment as a single unit. This is facilitated by modularity, where small units can be combined and recombined, or split off and reformed.

Work management solutions can be designed by creating a flow of modules that can be followed during execution, or they can be created on the fly through a series of decisions that are made at the time of execution.

Sidebar: The Theory of Constraints and CCPM

The following chapters cover the complex domain of project management.

The complex aspects of project management came into focus with the management philosophy of Dr. Eli Goldratt, the business guru behind the Theory of Constraints and Critical Chain Project Management (CCPM).

As we will see, many of the solutions offered in the following chapters are based on the ideas proposed by Goldratt.

Goldratt recognized the futility of trying to control everything in situations that were complex (i.e. that were inherently uncontrollable). His ideas therefore share a lot of similarities with CAS, including self-organization, simple rules, constraints, non-linearity, and sub-optimality.

For example, the crucial insight of TOC is that only a few elements (constraints) in a system control the results of the entire system. TOC tools identify these constraints, and focus the entire organization on simple, effective solutions to problems that seemed insurmountably complex and unsolvable. A very important corollary to this is that spending time optimizing non-constraints will not provide significant benefits; only improvements to the constraint will further the goal.

And yet, Critical Chain Project Management (CCPM) as a method of planning and managing projects has been extremely limited. So the obvious question to ask is: CCPM has been around for 30 years – why is it not more popular?

The reasons are many, starting with the unfortunate, uninspiring description of CCPM typified by Wikipedia:

> Critical chain project management (CCPM) is a method of planning and managing projects that emphasizes the resources (people, equipment, physical space) required to execute project tasks. It was developed by Eliyahu M. Goldratt. It differs from more traditional methods that derive from critical path and PERT algorithms, which emphasize task order and rigid scheduling. A critical chain project network strives to keep resources levelled, and requires that they be flexible in start times.

There is nothing in this definition that would remotely excite anyone, which is a good reason why CCPM is so misunderstood and rarely used. It also emphasizes resource leveling, which is the one thing we don't want from CCPM.

There are other reasons for the low impact of CCPM in the general project management world.

CCPM Literature is Not Easily Accessible to Typical Project Managers

There are some great bools out there on CCPM, but the simple message of CCPM is often drowned out by hundreds of pages of detailed analysis. These are not the kinds of books that the average project manager is going to wade through. Sometimes taking an idea at face value is all that is needed for it to be useful.

CCPM has Manufacturing Roots

A lot of the material on CCPM applies to manufacturing environments, since it is based on the Theory of Constraints (TOC), which was developed for manufacturing. It is likely to be off-putting for project managers in non-manufacturing environments.

CCPM Induces Discomfort

People grow comfortable with the old ways of doing things. They have been doing it this way for years. They are very good at doing it this way. Now you want them to change to do it a different way. Even if it's better, it takes them out of their comfort zone and all they see is more work.

CCPM Threatens Traditional Project Management

There are many project management consultants, and others who makes a living in project management education, who are invested in the perpetuation of traditional project management, and therefore have no interest in change.

CCPM is Counter-intuitive

CCPM cuts across decades of past experience and training, formal processes, customer demands, and performance.

Take these basic tenets, for example:

1. Allow team members to focus on their tasks sequentially rather than multi-tasking.
2. Reduce the amount of work in process.

3. Start tasks as late as possible.
4. It's okay for resources to be idle sometimes.
5. Remove all padding from individual tasks for the greater good.
6. Allow individual tasks to be late.
7. Not everything that is optimized has a positive effect on the organization.

CCPM is Not Needed Because "We Already Know How to Run Projects"

Project managers who have excellent track records based on hitting milestones don't think they need to change. However, simply hitting deadlines hardly tells the full story. Like cruise control, the project will speed up if it is running late (by team members working hard to get it back on track, sometimes working weekends and evenings to make it happen), or slow down if the project is early (people relax, maybe shuffling resources to something more urgent).

What had to take place to get there is hidden from view, and there is no impetus to finishing projects faster.

CCPM Applications are Too Complex

The existing crop of project management systems based on CCPM principles have been around for a long time. They are not for the faint of heart. They are also primarily aimed at humungous projects like building a Boeing 737. There is a lot of overkill for the kinds of projects we are talking about in this book.

Other Reasons

Other reasons include the following:

■ **Lack of awareness.** You cannot choose what you are unaware of. Remarkably few project managers have ever heard of CCPM.
■ **Improving throughput is not important.** Improving project throughput may not be highly valuable in all project environments. Cost management, for example, may be the factor which organizations are focusing on rather than project throughput.

- **It's "too hard".** Project managers have looked at CCPM and decided it would be too hard to implement in their environment.
- **Don't see the value.** Project managers don't believe CCPM has anything new or better to offer.
- **No constrained resources.** The organization has unlimited resources.
- **Resources not shared across projects.** Each project has its own set of resources.
- **Maybe it's *too* simple!** CCPM concepts are basic common sense. Sometimes it takes a beginner's mind to see the value. As Groucho Marx once said: "A child of five would understand this. Send someone to fetch a child of five."

A More Useful Definition of CCPM

A much more accurate definition of CCPM would be something along the lines of the following:

> Critical chain project management (CCPM) is a method of planning and managing projects that significantly increases the speed at which projects can be completed, by reducing the impact of negative behaviors, uncertainty, and limited resource availability.

Conclusion

As we will see in the next few chapters, the ideas behind CCPM, when applied properly, can be an incredibly powerful way to significantly improve project production, ease the lives of project managers, improve visibility over project status, and provide an early warning.

Notes

1. The Future is Podular – The Connected Company – Medium. https://medium.com/the-connected-company/the-future-is-podular-c71d090abf80.
2. The Future is Podular – The Connected Company – Medium. https://medium.com/the-connected-company/the-future-is-podular-c71d090abf80.

Chapter 7

Estimates

How Do You Accommodate Unpredictability, Variability, and Uncertainty in Task Estimates?

Every experienced manager knows that there is a high degree of variability in task durations. What many experienced project managers do not know is how this variability impacts overall project performance, and how the conventional approach of coping with variability unwittingly and unknowingly magnifies the damage.

At the root of this is the mistaken belief that variation averages out in projects. Yes, if all projects were linear, and resources were always available to work immediately when required, gains and delays would no doubt average out.

Unfortunately, most projects are not linear and resources are sometimes not available when needed. This gives rise to the Cascade Effect – every task that is late makes all the downstream tasks late.

Common Practice

Many of the problems with project management start right here:

Task estimates become commitments...

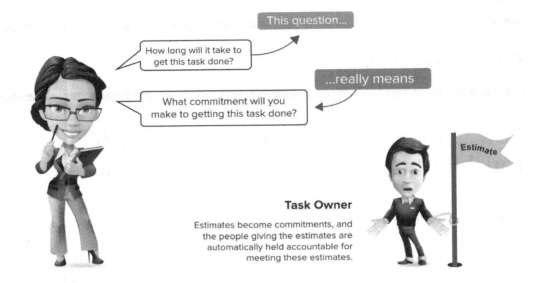

An estimate is not a prediction. We don't know how long anything will take. It is impossible to accurately estimate how long a step in a process or a task in a project takes, because there are so many variables. For example:

Task-level Contigency

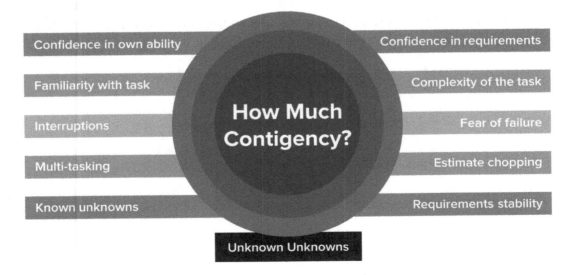

Given this uncertainty, if we want an accountable, committed date early on (something with 100 percent confidence that one can commit to), then the best anyone can do is to provide an estimate and then add some serious padding to the task in order to contend with the uncertainty and unknowns.

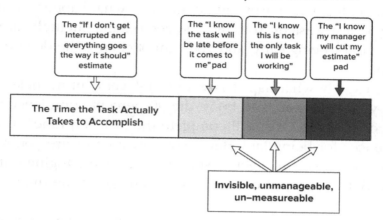

Common practice believes:

1. The best way to ensure that a project will finish on time is to make every task finish on time.
2. The best way to ensure that every task finishes on time is to add enough safety to task estimates to cover potential problems. For example:

You can't afford to miss your flight. How much time do you give yourself to make sure you get from your house to the airport on time?

1. The shortest time, with no traffic, is 20 minutes.
2. But on average, it takes 30 minutes.
3. However, if there is any kind of problem (construction, accident, weather, traffic), it could take as long as 60 minutes.

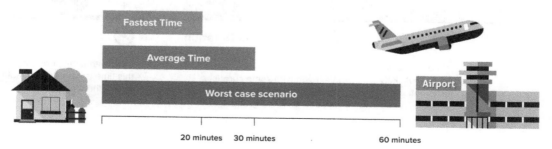

Which time do you choose?

Obviously, if you absolutely want to make sure you make your flight, you give yourself 60 minutes. Even then, you may not make it given extraordinary circumstances, but there is nothing you can do about that. But at 60 minutes, you have a 95 percent chance of being on time.

So you get lucky and arrive in 20 minutes. What happens to that extra 40 minutes you just wasted? Nothing. You get to hang out at the airport. There is no reward for being early, and you cannot change the departure time of your flight.

This is exactly what happens with task-level contingencies. The estimate you make needs to be in the 90 percent confidence range so that you can be sure you will complete the task "on time". There are consequences for being late. But if you finish early, are you rewarded? Probably not. Maybe you get to spend some time hanging out in the cafeteria. But the project cannot take advantage of the time you just saved.

So when a task owner is asked for an "estimate" (i.e. a commitment), they typically arrive at their number based on the following type of probability.

Which Time Are You Likely to Promise?

Probability of Task Duration Time

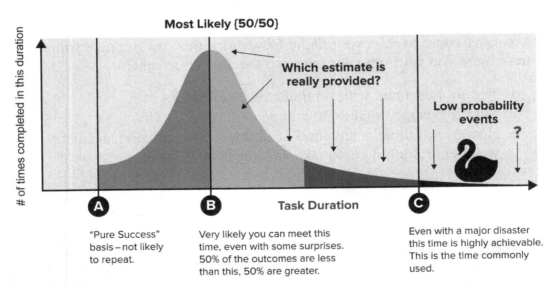

The Problem

The Size of Padding is Underestimated

When a "small" safety is added to estimates they are not considered unreasonable, because mentally we add safety assuming a normal distribution of time.

In a normal distribution, 50 percent of the time is to one side of the average and 50 percent of the time is to the other side of the average. Therefore, moving from a 50 peercent accuracy to 80 percent does not appear to be significant.

However, task times are not "normal". In fact, there is no such thing as "normal".

Task Times Do Not Follow a Normal Curve

Instead they start somewhere beyond zero (every task must take some amount of time) and then the probability of completing as promised ramps up quickly, only to drop off with a very long tail.

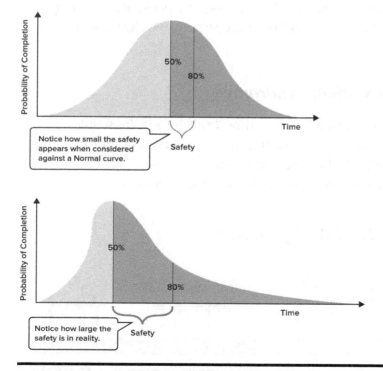

Figure 7.1   The higher the uncertainty the bigger the tail!

When you compare the two graphs you will see that the "small" safety time embedded is in reality quite large. The higher the uncertainty of the task the longer the tail grows.

Absolutely no one, of course, will admit that they do this. They'll say that they add, at most, 5 or 10 percent to their estimates, "just in case".

The incentives for this behavior are so deeply ingrained in the structure of the workplace that we don't even see them – there is constant pressure to add padding to estimates (to make sure we hit them), and no counter-pressure that would reward faster execution. Estimates in this environment become a self-fulfilling prophecy, always growing and never shrinking, discouraging anyone from taking advantage of opportunities for acceleration, even when they appear.

Task Estimates Become Commitments

The question *"How long will it take to get this task done?"* really means *"What commitment will you make to getting this task done?"*

Estimates become commitments and the people giving them are automatically held accountable for meeting these estimates.

But an estimate is not a commitment. It is a range of possibilities. There is no such thing as an accurate estimate! (If there was, it wouldn't be an estimate.)

Task Padding Leads to Student Syndrome

The knowledge that there is so much safety time built into tasks results in various time-wasting practices (e.g., waiting until the last moment to complete a task). As a result, all the safety time can be wasted at the start of the task so that, if problems are encountered, the task overruns.

Student Syndrome

Of course, this reflects the time wasted in the student world. In the business world there may be legitimate reasons why people will delay the start of a task because of other higher priority tasks. Nevertheless, the impact is the same.

The Impact of Task Padding is Much Worse than You Think

Even very high degrees of certainty about individual elements mean very little in terms of overall certainty. If we apply the rule of compound probability to the rest of the entire project, the answer gets much worse.

Just because each task has enough safety to ensure that there is a 95 percent chance of being on time, the probability of the project being late is not 95 percent.

For example:

1. If we set our estimates so that we are 90 percent sure that any one task will be completed on time;
2. If we have 20 tasks in our project;
3. The probability that all the tasks will be on time is: 0.9²⁰ = 12%;
4. For 50 tasks, the probability of all tasks on time is: 0.9⁵⁰ = 1%.
5. **So, for 50 tasks, there is a 99 percent probability of being late because at least one task will be late.** Of course, it's feasible that the time will be made up by later tasks, but given Student Syndrome and Parkinson's Law, this is unlikely.

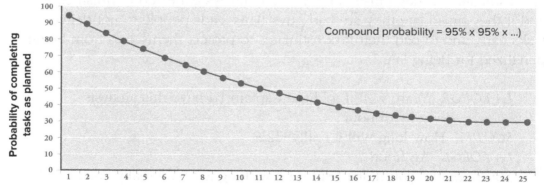

Compound probability of a series of tasks

Compound probability = 95% x 95% x ...)

Probability of completing tasks as planned

Number of tasks in series

Task Padding doesn't Accomplish what it's Supposed to do

Unfortunately, task padding gives a false sense of security, so the task is put off until the last moment.

When we plan to start the task

When we should finish if uninterrupted and no Murphy

This is time reserved for Murphy and management by crisis

Task Time | Safety

How it looks in our head when we add safety

When we should start

When we actually start due to Student Syndrome

When we hope to finish as long as Murphy doesn't strike

Safety | Task Time

How it actually happens

Task Padding Becomes Institutionalized

Late completion is penalized, causing a vicious circle. There is a tendency in organizations to "whack" people when they do not comply with their task estimates. If they finish early they are always expected to finish early, and if they finish late they are bad guys. This leads people to not deliver tasks early and to pad their task estimates to protect themselves from being penalized for being late.

> *LA FORGE:* Yeah, well, I told the Captain I'd have this analysis done in an hour.
> *SCOTTY:* How long will it really take?
> *LA FORGE:* An hour!
> *SCOTTY:* Oh, you didn't tell him how long it would really take, did ya?

LA FORGE: Well, of course I did.

SCOTTY: Oh, laddie. You've got a lot to learn if you want people
to think of you as a miracle worker.

Star Trek: The Next Generation: Relics (1992)

The Solution

The Aggregation Principle

The primary reason for task padding is to deal with uncertainty. In other
words, we are looking for insurance against things going wrong. The
solution to this problem is well known – aggregation of risk. This is the
basis for all insurance plans.

Insurance is designed to work by spreading costs across a large number
of people. Premiums are based on the average costs for the people in the
insured group. This risk-spreading function helps make insurance reasonably
affordable for most people.

Premiums that health care consumers   Money from the pot is used to pay the medical bills of people
pay go into the pot   in the risk pool who get sick

In terms of projects, we need to abandon the practice of trying to protect
each task and instead work to protect the overall project from the effects of
variability.

Buffers

Applying the idea of aggregation, the padding associated with each task is removed and put into a pool, called a buffer. Creating the pool of time at the end of the project doesn't extend the length of the project, because the pool comes from time removed from the individual tasks.

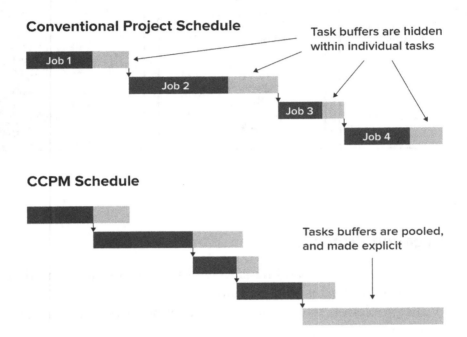

A buffer is analogous to a shock absorber in a car. Without suspension, the ride would be jarring and could result in damage to the car and its passengers. The amount of buffer required is a function of:

- The desired ride.
- The condition of the road.

So, if you want to make sure you get a smooth ride (projects are always completed on time), you need to make sure that the size of your buffer is capable of dealing with the condition of the road (the amount of uncertainty in the estimate).

In fact, when safety time is aggregated it can be significantly reduced and still provide a greater amount of protection. When risk is pooled, less total coverage is needed than if the risk is spread because not all takes are going to be late. Pooling project contingency typically requires about one-third less time contingency in order to stabilize a project timeline against uncertainty than when risk coverage is spread.

The project due date is protected as long as the accumulated lateness along any one critical path is less than the completion buffer.

How it Works

1. Estimates are done as usual.
2. The critical path is calculated (the longest series of tasks required to complete the project).
3. Each task estimate on the critical path is cut by 50 percent. This is "good enough" in most cases, but it can vary, however, based on the variability of the task. This becomes the "challenge time".
4. The other 50 percent is placed in the project buffer.

Once project managers set these buffers, they can monitor project health and timeliness by watching the buffer consumption rate rather than individual task completion to keep everything moving forward on schedule. This keeps a project manager from unnecessarily riding herd on feeding tasks that are running late, but that will not significantly impact the critical path.

Example

Here is how a contingency pool works in project management:

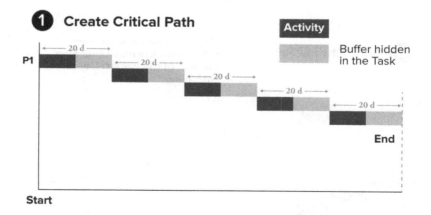

② **Reduce task durations by removing task buffers**

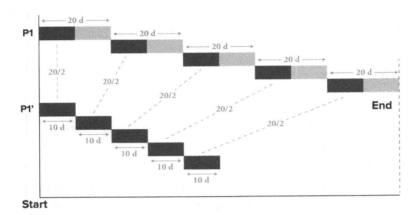

③ **Create a project buffer by removing the task buffers aggregating them at the end of the project**

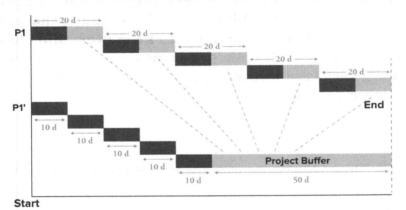

④ **New Critical Path**

"The uncertainly of the sum of the events is much less than the sum of the uncertainty for each event."

Critical Chain Project Management
Lawrence P. Leach

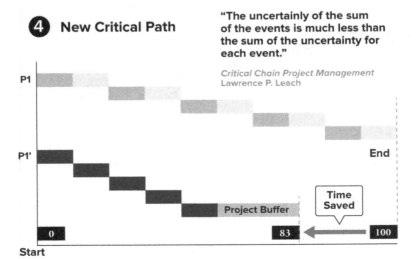

Project managers use the overall project buffer at the end of the project between the final task and the completion date to monitor project timeliness. Ideally, **delays on the longest chain of dependent tasks will eat away at the buffer but leave the completion date unchanged.** Unlike a traditionally managed project that has time buffers built into each task, the total project buffer allocated in a critical path will be smaller than the sum of all individual task buffer times of that traditionally managed project.

Milestone Buffers

If your organization uses milestones to judge project progress you can use a milestone buffer, which works in the same way as a project buffer.

Feeder Buffers

A potential delay in the critical path can be caused by late running "feeder" paths. Feeder paths are those tasks that are not on the critical path. A feeder buffer decouples a non-critical path from the critical path in order to prevent delays or late starts on the critical path due to late deliveries for non-critical tasks.

To protect progress, you can insert a feeder buffer between the last task on a feeder path and the critical path. The feeder buffer is created in exactly the same way as the project buffer.

If the feeder buffer looks late, you can reprioritize tasks on the feeder path so as not to delay the critical path.

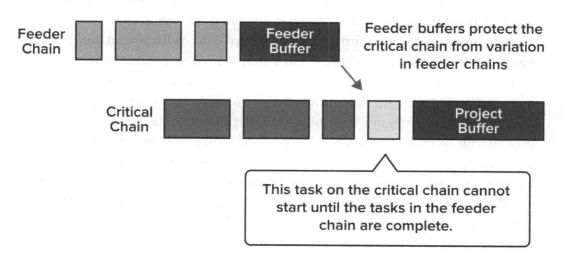

Feeder Chain

Feeder Buffer

Feeder buffers protect the critical chain from variation in feeder chains

Critical Chain

Project Buffer

This task on the critical chain cannot start until the tasks in the feeder chain are complete.

Convergence Buffers

Feeder buffers are particularly important when there are multiple paths that all converge at the same point in the critical path and any later steps can only start when all the preceding converging activities are complete.

Complex projects often fail because of a missed convergence due to unforeseen variation in the delivery of the preceding activities that are required.

To help ensure that all the paths to the convergence point arrive at the same time, it makes sense to create a milestone at the convergence point. The milestone provides a common point by which all the paths need to complete.

Benefits

Buffers can be used to manage a project through simple numerical measurements, which can be compared across projects. Analysis of buffer consumption allows project managers to focus their energies on the highest leverage tasks. This allows critical management time to be used more efficiently and helps avoid demoralizing micro-management. Management is encouraged not to micro-manage by the "green" buffer management area and to manage only high leverage tasks.

Buffers provide a simple means for communication both within and between projects. This can provide a global metric and help managers apply their limited resources on the tasks that will have the greatest impact on the money-making ability of the company.

Aggregated buffers encourage teamwork, which can lead to early task finishes. When the team shares an aggregated buffer and is primarily judged on overall project success, it promotes offloading non-essential tasks from the constrained resources. It also encourages early finishes so that the team can increase the project buffer. In addition, this change promotes constructive peer pressure. When a team shares an aggregated buffer, they are much more dependent on each other for success and will "push back" against teammates who unnecessarily waste the buffer. When resources have their own safety times, they feel that it is theirs to use, even if not needed. When the safety time is community property, the dynamic is completely different.

The focus on the small stuff is eliminated. We expect things to go wrong – if they never went wrong, we wouldn't need insurance (or a buffer). But because we have the project buffer we can stop worrying about every task, and just focus on how fast you are using up the buffer.

Less overall protection is needed. Not every task will be late. Individual tasks can be late without impacting the project completion date. With task buffers, if any task is later than its contingency allows, we have a problem. With a project buffer, we only have a problem if the total lateness exceeds the total contingency.

Projects can take advantage of tasks that come in ahead of time. They will replenish the buffer that was consumed by those that took longer than expected.

Student Syndrome is eliminated. There is no extra time available, so tasks must start immediately.

Parkinson's Law is eliminated. Work cannot expand to fit the time available, because there is no extra time to waste.

The three-minute egg syndrome is eliminated. No one will question early finishes. In fact, they will be rewarded.

The project buffer is visible, and therefore manageable. It provides the project manager with a clear indication of the health of the project at any point in time. The tracking of the consumption of these buffers provides warnings and indications of potential problems well before the project promise is in real trouble, allowing for the development of recovery plans in an atmosphere other than one of crisis.

There is a highly visible early warning of slippage. Using these buffers as protective "shock absorbers" safeguards the project from statistical fluctuation and resource contention. The project manager can use these newly developed measurements for early intervention, which will correctly focus management attention on tasks that keep the project on time and within budget.[1]

Figure 7.2   Not enough buffer.

Summary

Because traditional project management requires timely task completion to drive timely project completion, task estimates must be achievable regardless of variability. Therefore, the estimate must include a substantial amount of buffer/padding to accommodate this inevitable variability.

But not every task will require the task buffer allocated. As a result, much of this buffer is wasted. In addition, because people know there is a buffer built into their task, they may delay the start of the task (Student Syndrome), or delay reporting that it has been completed (Parkinson's Law).

Therefore, a better approach is to remove the buffers from individual tasks and aggregate them into a project buffer. This buffer pool can then be used by any task that needs it. In addition to reducing wasted buffers, the now aggressive amount of time allocated to tasks eliminates Student Syndrome and Parkinson's Law, among other benefits.

Note

1. Critical Chain | Method, Scheduling, Management. www.exepron.com/ critical-chain.

Chapter 8

Scheduling

How Do You Eliminate the Need for Constant Scheduling and Rescheduling of Tasks when Task Dates are Meaningless?

Task deadline scheduling is a classic example of a complicated solution being applied to a complex problem.

Dates and deadlines are the bedrock for all project and process monitoring. In theory, this makes perfect sense. Because certain tasks throughout your life have built-in deadlines it's tempting to think that everything needs one. In a way, deadlines are comforting, because they give you a concrete goal. You know what you need to do, and when you need to have it done by.

In theory.

But the reality is that when you assign deadlines to everything you do, a lot of them are arbitrary. A certain task doesn't need to be completed by a certain time – you just tell yourself that it does as a way of holding yourself accountable. Which might not be a problem, except for the fact that not all deadlines are arbitrary – and fake ones can get in the way of real ones. Separating the things that need to be done on deadline from the things that don't gets confusing, and that's where the problems really start.[1]

Deadlines get moved around so much because only a few of them actually matter.

This means that you're constantly moving things around on your calendar, trying to find the perfect way to squeeze everything into place in a way that makes sense, when most of those things don't actually need to be squeezed in at all.

When you only set deadlines for things that actually need them, you're free to prioritize the rest of your projects as needed – and it's a lot easier to keep them organized than you may think. It's a lot easier to solve a jigsaw puzzle with 100 pieces than one with 10,000 pieces.[2]

Common Practice

The way to ensure that the project will finish on time is to make sure every task finishes on time. The underlying theory is that if all the tasks completed on time, the project will be completed on time.

So projects are managed by carefully watching the calendar, comparing where we are today against some baseline schedule. That schedule typically consists of a series of start and due dates for consecutive tasks, with due dates of predecessors matching start dates of successors. Like a train schedule, if a task arrives at its completion on or before its due date, that portion of the project is considered to be "on track".

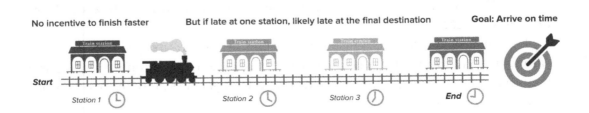

The Problem

Task deadlines cause a significant number of problems, many of which are underestimated in their impact.

- Due dates add another thing to manage, add rigidity, and take constant energy to hold.
- Due dates are an added stress – the weight of a looming deadline
- Due dates allow us to pretend that reality is more predictable and controllable than it actually is.
- Due dates cause people to relax in a sense of certainty.

Since task scheduling is a fundamental component of traditional project management, it is worth delving into the problems it causes.

Task deadlines change. Right from the start, in attempting to impose a rigid construct on a variable situation, we have in effect planned to fail. Why? Because actual dates will *always* change. Task deadlines are based on estimates and are therefore impossible to predict with accuracy. They are also dependent on factors like resource availability and predecessors not completing on time. Therefore, attempting to run a project by task scheduling is not possible and doing so by trying to keep task deadlines constantly updated is an exercise in futility. Not only is the amount of time dedicated by project managers to this activity excessive, it also distracts them from focusing on far more important things in managing the project.

Time spent on deadline scheduling has rapidly diminishing returns. It's tempting to believe the mantra "plan, plan, plan". Since it's

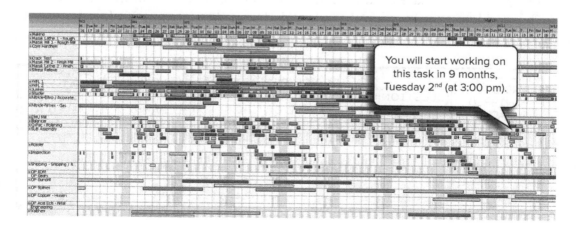

impossible to account for every possible contingency for every single task at a certain point, it becomes counter-productive to keep planning.

Giving task deadlines that cannot be met wastes project managers' time and encourages wrong behavior. Due dates introduce the risk that I will end up working on something so as to meet a commitment – often an artificial commitment – regardless of whether it is the most important thing I should be working on, given the project's broader purpose.

Due dates lead to unconsciously chasing deadline commitments instead of consciously selecting and working on the most important action in every moment. Giving someone a due date does not make that action the most important thing to do.

There is no potential for early delivery. While it is important for trains to arrive at and depart from their stations (their milestones) at appointed times, the value of a project is more often tied to the absolute speed from beginning to end. The sooner the entire project is completed, the sooner project benefits can be accrued.

Deadline conformance is not a good measurement of people. If the dates are arbitrary, or negotiated, or conceal a lot of variability, it's far better to measure people based on how they really do (e.g. quality and speed of work, attitude) rather than their ability to hit dates.

Task deadlines become self-fulfilling prophecies, at least in terms of expectations of speed. They may still (and often do) take longer due to being derailed by Murphy's Law because they have wasted what might have been early finishes which are now not available to offset tasks that take longer than anticipated.

Deadline scheduling causes late starts by workers. Even if workers are given a start date for a task, they typically only focus on the end date. The problem occurs when the scheduled start time arrives. It often happens

that there is other "urgent stuff" on one's desk when the task shows up in the in-box. And in any event, we have until the promised date to finish the work, which at this point looks like a long way off due to the safety time included in the estimate. We are comfortable putting off or "pacing" the work in favor of other stuff because the due date is out there.

The "urgent stuff" takes precedence until we see the due date sneaking up on us, or, as the following graphic shows, the due date is within even the aggressive expected duration of the work itself. Sometimes it sneaks up quietly enough (drowned out by the louder squeaking wheels) so that when we look, we realize that it has now become urgent and gets our attention.

The safety time we included was not only for the non-project distractions but also for the unknowns (the "Murphy") associated with the task itself. We cannot know what problems will crop up until we start the work. And we've started the work later than planned, after eating up most, if not all, of our safety time attending to other important work. There isn't time left to recover from the problems in time to meet the due date, at least not without heroics, burnout, or loss of quality.[3]

Deadline scheduling encourages project managers to get tasks started before they are ready to be started. Just as adding more work-load will not lead to more accomplishment, rushing task initiation will not automatically lead to faster completion. Under pressure to show progress against deadlines, managers will often start tasks before they and their

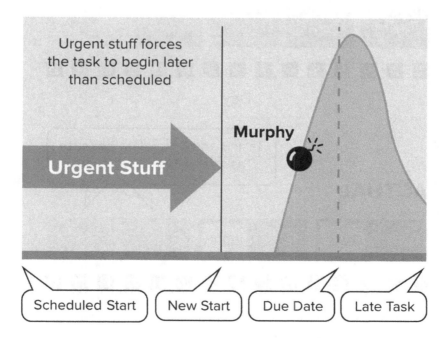

teams have all the necessary information, and tools they need to complete the work. These false starts are more than nuisances – they are obstructions with significant consequences:

■ Deceleration – As partially finished work clogs the work flow, every project takes longer and longer to fulfill.
■ False assumptions – When project members don't have all the information they need, they make project decisions based on available data, resulting in poor outcomes.
■ Rework – If the previous assumptions were indeed incorrect, partially completed work will need to be redone, creating additional costs and delays.

Deadline scheduling leads to cascading delays. Early finishes are not propagated through the project at all, but delays are always propagated! If just one of the tasks on the critical path is late, the whole schedule gets pushed out.

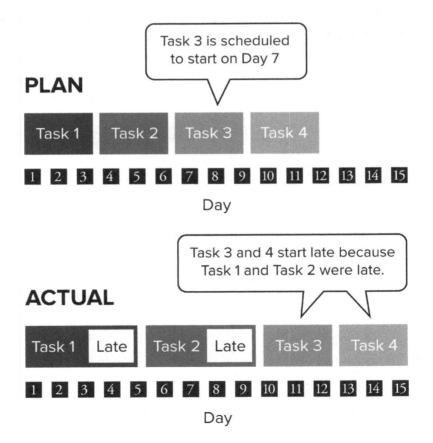

Since early task finishes don't materialize, any task that is late has no offset, thereby making project end-date slip almost inevitable. The cumulative effect of taking away the possibility of finishing tasks early is devastating to the chances of completing a project on time.

Cascading delays are inevitable. In the absence of perfect clarity,and 100 percent predictability, disturbances at one task in a project will ripple into other tasks.

Early finishes are rarely reported. Most seasoned project managers know that tasks either finish on time or late, but almost never finish early. A key contributing factor: the system of rewards and punishments and how they are applied. When a worker finishes a task early, what happens? There is no reward for finishing early. When the tasks are ahead of schedule, no one pays attention, so there is no incentive to complete the task early.

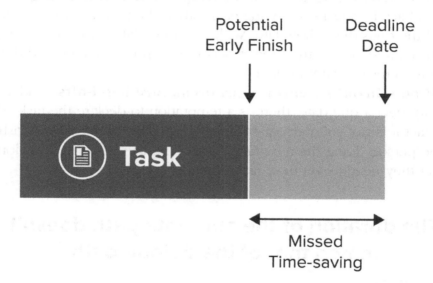

There are many other reasons that early finishes are not reported:

- **Eroded negotiating position.** You don't want the early finish to become the new expectation.
- **Resentment.** Other workers may resent a team member finishing early because it makes their time estimates for similar tasks look bad. The early finisher in effect is taking away others' safety by showing management that the task can be done faster than consensus shows it can be done.

- **Three-minute egg rule.** It's not quality if it's finished before the time is up. As a result, deadline scheduling does not take advantage of early finishes.
- **Eroded credibility.** You don't want your credibility questioned. As a result, deadline scheduling does not take advantage of early finishes.

Deadline scheduling defuses focus. Tracking individual task deadlines results in an ever-increasing fog of information as the project progresses. What makes this problem worse is the constant need to shuffle the schedule owing to date changes, as well as the lack of distinction between critical and non-critical tasks. With so much detail to track, project managers struggle to analyze data and transform it into useful information that can drive focused decision making.

Deadline scheduling guarantees frequent schedule changes. Since the plan is based on tasks following each other, the first task that is late makes all the ones that follow late. With no buffer, later tasks are forced to make up any slide. So, the project becomes a moving target, and the schedule requires constant updating.

Deadline scheduling encourages premature hand-offs. Under pressure to meet a due date, there is a temptation to declare the task "done" when in fact it is not 100 percent complete. It pushes problems downstream, where the person doing the next task risks being late because they don't have what they need to get their task done on time.

The duration of the alternate path doesn't match that of the default path

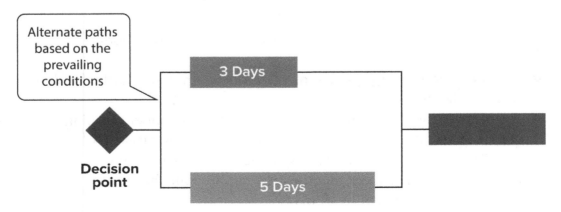

Deadline scheduling hides the level of lateness. The level of lateness is sometimes hard to identify clearly, because when it is obvious that dates will be missed they often change. The date is no longer considered late if the date is moved out.

Deadline scheduling makes conditional path scheduling difficult. If you have conditional paths in your project plan, task deadlines make no sense, because you don't know which path will be taken, and therefore which tasks will be executed by what date.

Deadline scheduling fosters "schedule chicken". People are reluctant to report that they are going to miss their deadline. But they will not have to do so if someone else reports a delay first and thereby takes the blame for the project being late. This may result in serious problems until it's too late to recover from them.

Deadline scheduling leads to multi-tasking. Starting work as early as possible, even when not scheduled, is a response to worst-case estimates. When workers give worst-case estimates, they don't expect to stay busy with just one task – so they multi-task, working on several tasks at once by

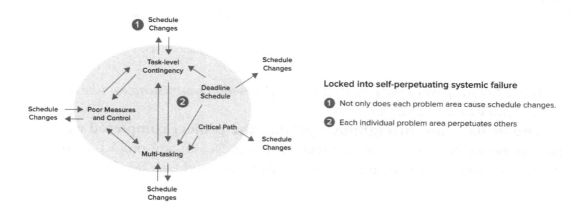

switching between them. The result is that everything takes a long time to complete and very little completes early.[4]

Deadline scheduling is self-perpetuating.

The Solution

> The solution is not about removing due dates – it's about improving the way work gets done such that due dates for tasks become irrelevant.

A Relay Race Ethos

The solution is to run your project like a relay race rather than a train track. In a relay race, resources are encouraged to pick up the input hand-off as soon as it is available, "run with it" in a full, focused, sustainable level of effort, and hand off the output as soon as it is complete. Team members are asked to dedicate themselves to a project task, to complete it as quickly as possible, and to periodically report how many days are remaining.

The baton is passed along the chain of tasks and their participants. What is far more important than the date of the handover is the will of everyone to complete the overall race in the shortest reasonable and possible time.

| Great incentive to finish faster (beat your best time!) | Make sure the next runner is ready when the previous runner completed | Goal: Arrive as quickly as possible |

Start — Runner 1 — Runner 2 — Runner 3 — End

But it's ok if you slow down due to unforeseen circumstances, like bumpy track or bad weather.

But it's okay if you slow down due to unforeseen circumstances, like a bumpy track or bad weather

The focus is on throughput – getting the project completed as fast as possible. It encourages a relay race mindset among project team members rather than utilizing rigid task scheduling and task deadlines.

How it Works

1. **The relay race is defined by the critical path.** This is the longest chain of tasks through the project at any given point in time. The critical path makes clear which tasks need to be focused on to complete a project in time. Any day of slippage on a critical path task will cause slippage on the overall project. The critical path may change frequently when the project is emergent – when tasks are decided only during the course of the project. This is okay, since the system will automatically recalculate the critical path so that it's always clear which tasks are critical and need to be completed as quickly as possible. The critical path becomes the guide for allocation of resources and prioritization. Tasks on the critical path obviously get a higher priority than tasks not on the critical path.

2. **Task due dates are neither given nor monitored.** The completion of each task determines the start of the next step instead of using dates to determine when tasks start. This is what you do anyway when you keep on changing the dates to match reality. So why not let the system do it for you?

3. The system provides a heads-up notification to the person responsible for the following step by constantly monitoring step completions. The output of a step needs to be handed over to the next person assigned to the follow-up task. This is "running the relay race".

Management by Priority

Since individual task dates don't matter, dates don't drive the priority.

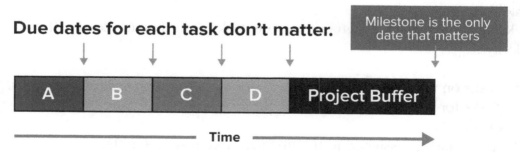

Variation in the task dates leading up to the project date are accommodated by the project buffer. No need to change the schedule.

Task dates are therefore eliminated and replaced by management by priorities, rather than management by date.

Instead of task schedules planned up front, you need a simple task prioritization process that can be applied in real time.

Sally's Task List		
To do	*Priorities*	~~*Due Date*~~
Task A	1	~~Tuesday~~
Task C	2	~~Thursday~~
...		

Clear, stable priorities help people focus attention where it's needed and reduce multi-tasking.

There are many factors that can be considered in prioritizing tasks, including how the tasks impact project endpoints, the relative priority of the tasks' projects, and the current status of those projects. But these are more relevant than arbitrary dates that keep on changing.

A Global Focus

The only solution to conflicting priorities is to set up a single, global priority system, not arbitrarily chosen by individual resources or imposed by competing managers but determined by the overall project goals and deadline.

Resource managers assign and execute tasks according to the global priority:

1. Tasks on the critical path are always done before non-critical path tasks.
2. Tasks for projects falling behind are given priority if there is an overlap.
3. A new task is assigned to the first available resource (after finishing the previous task).

For multiple projects, the most important task is likely to be the one that must be executed for the project under the greatest threat. The threatened project is not necessarily the one with the most remaining tasks before completion but the project most at risk of falling behind.

Implications

Individual task dates become much less important. Removing task contingencies and providing project contingency reduces the amount of time taken to plan and maintain detailed task dates. The focus shifts from task estimates to assuring the only date that matters – the final promised due date of a project.

Users don't clock themselves against a scheduled finish date – they just finish as fast as possible, focusing on appropriate quality and without fear of calling out issues that need to be addressed.

Resource performance is based on the efficiency and effectiveness of getting the task completed. They are given an aggressive task duration based on how long it would take for a dedicated resource to complete the task as a goal, but it is understood by the resource and management that there are things beyond their control that may impact the speed at which they can get things done. They will thus be highly motivated not to multi-task nor to delay getting started, nor wait to report things getting done.

Benefits

Finish projects faster. The problem with this common practice is that while it is important for trains to arrive at and depart from their stations at appointed times, project value is more often tied to the absolute speed from beginning to end. The sooner the entire project is completed, the sooner project benefits can be accrued.

Take advantage of early finishes. If resources run their leg of the relay race in an effective and efficient manner, some tasks will take longer than anticipated in the schedule and some will take less time. The project is in a position to take full advantage of early finishes. In this way, the cumulative risk associated with due-date behaviors is replaced by the consumption and replenishment of buffers.[5]

Individual tasks can be late. Individual tasks can now be late without affecting the completion date of the project. The project date is protected as long as the accumulated lateness along any one critical path is less than the

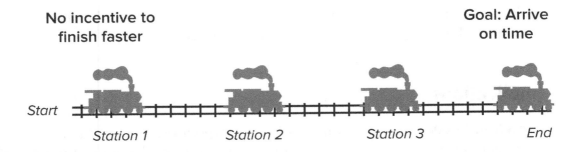

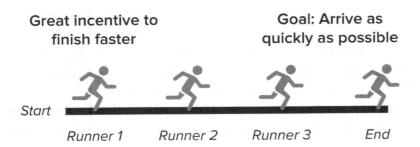

completion buffer. Over the course of the project we expect our buffers to be used up, in proportion to progress made.

Schedule stability. Using a project buffer significantly reduces the need to change the schedule. As long as there is a buffer available, there is no need to change milestone or project end dates.

Reduced multi-tasking. Participants assigned tasks on the critical path have a single priority – the current task to which they are assigned. Without

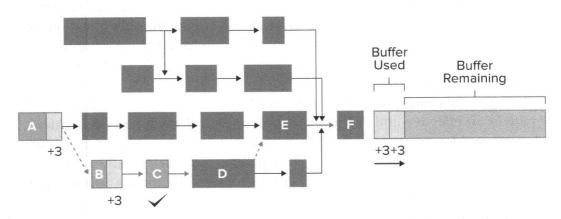

Tasks A and B took longer than expected, but Task C was on time.

There is no need to change the schedule. The number of additional days are simply subtracted from the project buffer.

the distraction of pressures to multi-task or to meet false priorities of task due dates, they can concentrate on the task and "just do it", do just it, and do it justice to assure a quality hand-off, successful projects, and maximum throughput for the organization.

Put the focus on work, not on dates. Buffers are used to absorb that variation without distraction to the resource performing the task at hand, while at the same time protecting the truly critical promises of the project. The result is the elimination of meaningless intermediate task due dates and the detrimental pressures, behaviors, and practices associated with them. Using the relay race ethos, you are spared the burden of keeping your eye on the calendar – you simply get the task done as quickly as possible.[6]

It solves the conditional path problem. By using the relay race approach the individual task dates don't matter, so it doesn't matter which path the process goes down.

Summary

When task buffers are eliminated, task deadlines become irrelevant. Only the project deadline matters.

The project completion date is determined by how quickly work on the critical path can be completed. To do this, projects are run like a relay race along the critical path rather than like stops in a train schedule. As soon as a person starts a critical task (a task on the critical path), they try to get it completed as quickly as possible rather than focusing on some arbitrary deadline. Once completed, the next task in the critical path sequence is automatically started, regardless of dates. In this way, the critical path is traversed as quickly as possible, instead of being constrained by task deadlines.

Priorities set by the project manager determine the sequence in which a person works on their tasks if they have been allocated more than one task at a time. In this way, there is no need to attempt to schedule task start and completion dates on the critical path.

Notes

1. Why We Stopped Assigning Deadlines – And What Happened. https://meetedgar.com/blog/why-we-stopped-assigning-deadlines-and-started-getting-more-done-because-of-it/.
2. Why We Stopped Assigning Deadlines – And What Happened. https://meetedgar.com/blog/why-we-stopped-assigning-deadlines-and-started-getting-more-done-because-of-it/.
3. In Most Projects Estimates are Turned into a Project. www.coursehero.com/file/p3hgp5/In-most-projects-estimates-are-turned-into-a-project-schedulea-list-of/.
4. Critical Chain Project Management – NPD Solutions. www.npd-solutions.com/critical.html.
5. CiteSeerX — CriticalChain and RiskManv/DvD. http://citeseerx.ist.psu.edu/viewdoc/summary?doi=10.1.1.5.8093.
6. Program Management – TOC Multi-project Management. www.projectsmart.co.uk/white-papers/turning-many-projects-into-few-project-priorities-with-toc.pdf.

Chapter 9

Execution

How Can You Ensure that Projects are Completed as Quickly as Possible in a Complex Multi-project Environment with Shared Resources?

The critical need to streamline work-in-progress is to maximize the flow of projects through the delivery pipeline. Local measures, such as how quickly a project gets started or how fully utilized resources are, are not valuable to the goals of the organization.[1]

Rather, the throughput of the entire organization, global optimization, should be the focus.

A Holistic Perspective

The core problem of project portfolio management isn't planning (or budgeting); it's directing shared resources to the right projects at the right time in a constantly changing environment.

Most project environments do not have the luxury of being able to focus on only one effort – they are usually multi-project environments, where key resources are shared across projects and have to compete for their attention.

As a result, while a particular single project may be carefully planned, with effective risk management applied within its borders, it may still be subject to programmatic risk, particularly related to availability of resources that are involved in other, equally important projects.

So even with safeguards at the individual project and task level, the pressures to jump from a task on one project to another – to multi-task across projects – can still be overwhelming and distracting if resources are faced with an overflowing in-box of tasks clamoring for their attention.[2]

It is therefore necessary to look beyond the individual projects, or even pairs of them, to the larger system encompassed by the organization responsible for accomplishing many projects.

Common Practice

In multi-project organizations, projects are often launched without sufficient regard for the capacity of the organization.

The Sooner We Get Started, The Sooner We'll Finish!

It seemingly makes sense: starting projects as soon as possible will get them completed as fast as possible.

We Need to Take Advantages of New Opportunities!

In an effort to take advantage of valuable new opportunities, more often than not, multi-project organizations tend to launch projects as soon as they are understood, concurrently with other projects, simultaneously with other new efforts.

We Need to Keep Our Resources Busy!

Work gets pushed into and through the system by the desire for high utilization of workers. The underlying assumption is that anything less than high utilization of every worker represents a lost opportunity for production.

The Problem

When the number of resources remains static, increasing volume of work in process merely increases confusion, increases conflict – and decreases real productivity.

Production throughput is a function of system capacity. If a system has more work to do than it is capable of handling, it quickly grinds to a halt. This is like what happens when your computer hits 100 percent capacity.

Work-in-progress (in the form of started but unfinished projects) quickly clogs up the system.

This happens when projects are pushed into the organization without regard for the system's capacity and capability.

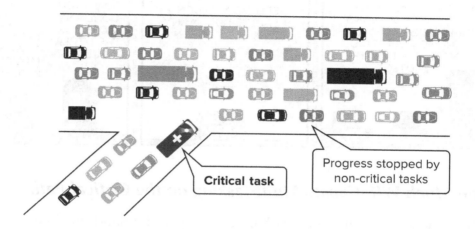

Critical task

Progress stopped by non-critical tasks

The obvious problem with too much WIP is that it slows down throughput:

- The build-up of work-in-process creates queues of work that dilute and diffuse the time and attention of resources and management alike.
- Having too much to deal with at any one time makes it harder to see problems hidden beneath the surface. It also impacts the ability to respond to change.

This is when individuals start to work independently on what they presume are their priorities when uncertainties unfold and individuals can no longer follow the original schedules. By definition, such independently set priorities are unsynchronized, causing a project to be mostly waiting for something or other. For example:

- Waiting for resources because they have been assigned to other tasks;
- Waiting for specifications, approvals, materials, etc. because the supporting resources that were supposed to supply or obtain these things were busy elsewhere;

- Waiting for issues to get resolved because experts are righting other issues;
- Waiting for decisions because managers have too much on their plates;
- Waiting for all feeding legs of the project to come together at integration points.

Too Much WIP Causes Multi-tasking on the Critical Path

Since true progress in a project happens only at the hand-offs between resources (i.e. when the work completed by one resource allows another resource to start its work), multi-tasking results in delays and unpredictable completion times (it is impossible to know how long one task takes when it is competing for a worker's time and attention with many other tasks).

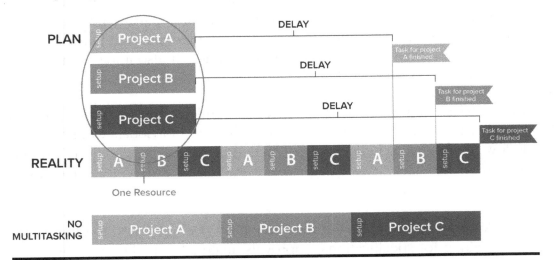

Figure 9.1   To the extent that one project's tasks are interrupted by work being performed on other projects' tasks, the first project is delayed.

If a resource divides its attention between different tasks before handing off task deliverables, all the projects involved will take longer than necessary because all of that resource's successors on each project will have to wait longer than necessary due to time spent on other projects' work. The projects will also be impacted by the variability of not only their own tasks but also of those associated with the other projects that are interleaved within them.

The pressures of these competing priorities result in the splitting of attention and energy, loss of focus, and inability to complete tasks and projects in a timely manner, or even within the time in which they were planned – at least without heroic efforts. This is not a desirable outcome for projects that want to keep their promises, or for organizations that need to reliably deliver projects in shorter and shorter intervals.[3]

Support Resources Become Overloaded

You don't find these resources in the project plan – they are dealing with all the situations that cannot be planned for. They manage and support project work as needed. Therefore, their workload is a function of the number of projects that are active. The greater the WIP, the higher the workload! The best way to exploit the capacity of experts and support resources is to keep the number of active projects low so that these resources can make the rest of the organization productive.

Decreased Productivity

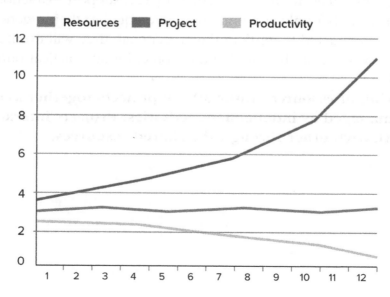

When the number of resources remains static, increasing the volume of work-in-progress merely increases confusion, increases conflict – and decreases real productivity.

While everyone looks busy, the true picture often remains obscure until deadlines approach, when the failure to complete projects becomes all too visible.

The Solution

One of the ways to reduce complexity is to reduce the number of variables, interrelationships, etc. that have to be dealt with at any one time.

So when an organization activates too much project work, the ultimate negative effect is that project execution is delayed, resulting in the project benefits being significantly delayed, reduced, or eliminated.

The problem is that there is no mechanism in place to prevent this from happening.

The Need for Flow

Non-renewable resources are stock limited. The entire stock is available at once, extracted at any rate, limited mainly by extraction. But since the stock is not renewed, the faster the extraction rate, the shorter the lifetime of the resource.

Renewable resources are flow limited. They can support extraction or harvest indefinitely but only at a finite flow rate equal to their regeneration rate. If they are extracted faster than they regenerate they will eventually be driven below a critical threshold and become, for all practical purposes, non-renewable.[4]

The sharing of resources links all the projects together and they cannot be managed as independent activities. Projects interact directly with each other through the shared resources.

The Concept of Flow

The neck of the funnel determines the rate of flow

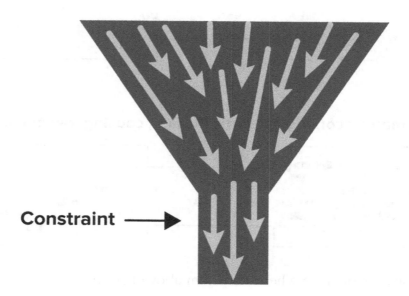

Constraint ⟶

If a paper shredder has been designed to handle 5 pages at a time and you have 100 pages to shred, attempting to feed all 100 pages at once is impossible. Feeding anything more than 5 pages at a time will just jam the machine and increase the time each page takes to be shredded, as well as the total time it would take to shred all 100 pages. The fastest way to shred all 100 pages is to control the number of pages you feed into the machine.[5]

No system (organization, machine, person) has infinite capacity. There is always a constraint; otherwise your production would be limitless. While a shredder will come with instructions that tell you what the shredder constraint is, it's usually not that simple.

If we think of the organization's total set of project portfolio resources as a busy stretch of highway, and we think of projects as flowing through the organization like cars traveling on that highway, then maximizing portfolio throughput would be equivalent to maximizing how many cars can travel that stretch of highway over a given period of time.

The question is: "What is the optimal number of cars to allow onto the freeway to achieve peak traffic flow?"

Few cars = fast throughput, but low density
(number of cars through the system)

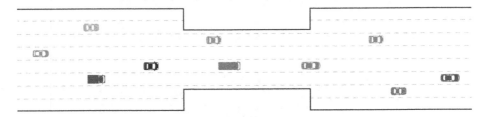

Too many incoming cars = traffic jam, causing low density

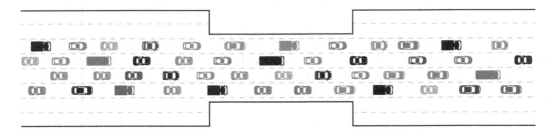

The answer is obvious when seen from above like this:

Peak traffic flow is equal to the capacity of the bottleneck

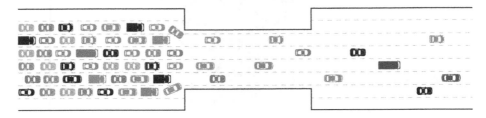

Limiting WIP

So, while speed is important, and adding capacity may well be in order, the first thing that needs to be done is to get traffic to flow.

Just fixing this one problem can produce significant improvements in production.

In the same way, the solution is to find a way to pipeline projects into the system so that it is not overloaded. This is how traffic flow is controlled:

a meter limits the on-ramp traffic in a way that keeps the highway traffic flowing.

Cars entering the freeway are staggered so as not to clog up the freeway, delaying everyone.

In the project management world, this is called project staggering or pipelining. Effective multi-project management requires the staggering of projects in a way that does not put strain on the resources available to the organization yet maximizes organizational throughput.

This is a factor that is rarely considered, yet it often has the most impact on how quickly projects can get done.

The question is: How do you find the constraint limiting production? What is the system capacity?

The Theory of Constraints (TOC)

> TOC is a thinking process that enables people to invent simple solutions to complex problems.
> *Eliyahu Goldratt, creator of the Theory of Constraints*

Theory of Constraints (TOC) is a holistic or systems-oriented approach to process improvement. It identifies the few things (constraints) that make a difference in a system.

TOC is based on the CAS understanding that complex systems exhibit inherent simplicity: that in any complex system at any point in time there is only one, or, at most, very few aspects of the system keeping that system from achieving more of its goal. So, even a very complex system made up of thousands of people and pieces of equipment can have at any given time only a very small number of variables that actually limits the ability to generate more of the systems goal.

These constraints, if properly identified and broken, provide the fastest route to significant improvement of the system and can provide the basis for long-term, strategic improvement.

The corollary to this is that conventional wisdom which calls for lots of process improvements in areas that cannot optimize the enterprise are a waste of time. Indeed, conventional wisdom does not even acknowledge the system constraint, let alone target it for improvement.

Although there can be more than one scarce type of resource, there can only be one scarcest resource.

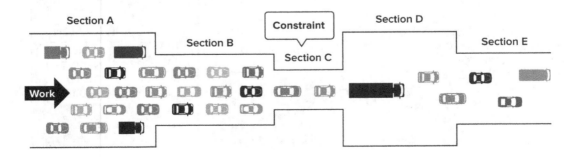

Once a constraint is no longer a constraint, it means the constraint has moved on to a different part of the system.

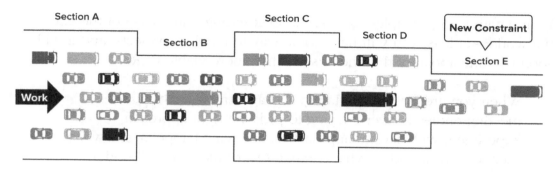

In a manufacturing environment, the constraint may be the number of robots on the assembly line, or of a specific type of robot on the assembly line. In services, the constraint is the number and kinds of resources available at any specific time.

What is the constraint in your organization that governs system capacity?

The Critically Constrained Resource (CCR)

It's much easier to manage a portfolio of projects when you only need to pay close attention to those few things.

Decisions become easier because the health of the constraint indicates how well the portfolio is doing. If the constraint is limping, the portfolio is limping. If it's well, all is well. The focus is on the resources that drive sharing across the projects. In a medical setting, the constrained resource may be something like the surgeon resource pool.

Every situation will be different, but there are a few criteria to consider when looking for the critically constrained resources; for example:

- *Define the boundaries of the system*
  Obviously, if you have a project with many phases running over multiple years, it doesn't make sense to look for a CCR across the entire project.
- *Limit the timeframe*
  Typically, you won't want to look more than six months out, and you should limit the boundaries to where there is an identifia-ble CCR. When we say "portfolio throughput", we are specifically

referring to how many project completions an organization can achieve over a given period of time.

In line with CAS principles, getting the CCR wrong initially is not the end of the world – at least you will have some way to pipeline projects, and it will soon become apparent that there is another, more viable CCR.

> When you are far from certainty and agreement, rather than meeting endlessly over it trying to pick the right approach, experiment with several approaches. See what happens, see what seems to work and in what context. Over time, you will find a right way for you, or you may find several right ways.
> *Brenda Zimmerman, Curt Lindberg, and Paul Plsek, Edgeware: Lessons from Complexity Science for Health Care Leaders (2001, Plexus Institute)*

For projects, the critical path (the series of steps that determine the minimum time needed for the project) is the primary constraint. No matter how quickly the other tasks get completed, the project cannot be finished any sooner unless the tasks on the critical path can be done sooner. This is obviously not a constraint that can leveraged.

The constraint for projects that *can* be leveraged is the availability of the right types of resources being available at the right time to those tasks on the critical path. Of these resources, typically only one type of those resources will be the most constrained resource. This is called the Critically Constrained Resource (CCR).

Instead of starting projects as soon as possible, independent of all other projects in the pipeline, the staggering of projects through the resource constraint helps make the interdependency visible for all projects in the pipeline.

The next question that we need to answer now is: "How do we operate the system to achieve maximum throughput?"

Finding the Constraint

The first step is to identify the resource that is commonly used across projects and relatively heavily used compared to other resources. Critically constrained resources are those who typically have the highest workload and the fewest resource numbers.

In some organizations the constraint is obvious. For example, in a medical setting, the constrained resource may be something like the surgeon resource pool:

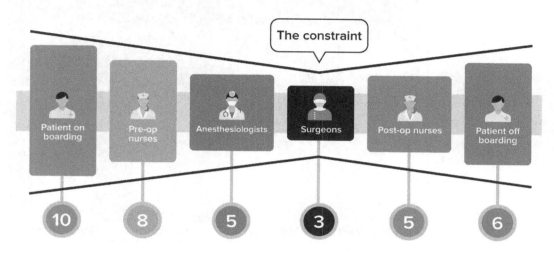

Capacity: Number of concurrent patients each department can handle

The constraint could be a specific resource, resource pool, group, etc., the capacity of which cannot be easily increased (e.g. it may be expensive, difficult to get, or cannot be easily outsourced); a recurrently overloaded resource or resource pool producing peaks and troughs within the project flow destroying the working pace; or a visible waiting queue or bottleneck in the project flow. The root cause will be the constraint.

There are a number of ways to identify the constraint (other than by manager intuition):

- Where is there a work backlog?
- Where do most problems occur?
- Which resources or tasks require the most management attention?
- Which resources are heavily utilized?
- Which resource is strategic and whose capacity cannot easily be augmented, is expensive, difficult to get, or cannot be easily outsourced?
- Which resources are used by the majority of the projects? Choose a resource that should be an internal constraint at peak time.

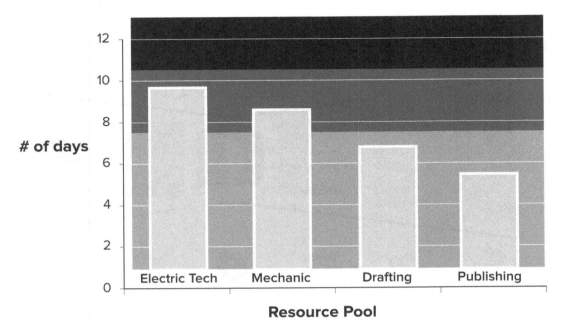

Average number of days a task is waiting for this resource

While there will always be constrained resources, it is possible that there is no clear limiting resource. There are other possibilities that can be considered. For example, the constraint could be a policy such as limiting the number of projects in execution at one time and not starting a new one until another is complete.

The question becomes: "How many projects can our organization handle effectively and efficiently at the integration point?"

The key is that you have to find a way to stagger (pipeline) the introduction of new projects into the system so you don't have too much WIP and overload your resources.

Pipeline Projects

The intention of pipelining projects is not about starting projects as soon as possible, it is about getting more projects completed.

Minimizing Risk of Cross-project Impacts

In a multi-project environment with shared resources, the effectiveness of individual projects can be threatened if the organization tries to push more projects through its pipeline than it is capable of. Scheduling – the actual promising of individual project completions – must take into account any constraining aspects of that pipeline.

Concentrating resources on fewer projects at one time allows teams to focus and reduces multi-tasking. This not only allows projects to be executed faster but creates capacity to undertake more initiatives.

Organizations that can successfully focus everyone's attention on the few, critically important goals rather than getting pulled into the tyranny of the urgent can create a significant strategic advantage over their competitors. Organizations that are successful with this strategy can be a highly productive, harmonious, collaborative, and innovative entity that operates within a sustainable, high-trust environment.

The Role of the Synchronizer

1. Once you have identified the most constrained resource, you stagger the introduction of projects based on the availability of that resource.
2. By identifying the constraint you've identified your true project capacity, making it easier to determine which and how many projects you can take on and the best sequencing of your projects.
3. The critically constrained resources become the "synchronizer" – the factor or resource used to determine when a new project can be scheduled. The role of the synchronizer is to set the pace at which projects are launched into the system. The synchronizer is sometimes referred to as the "drum" – it acts as the drumbeat of the organization.
4. Once the pacing resource has been identified, projects are released into the pipeline according to the capacity of the CCR and the prioritization of the project portfolio.
5. They provide a stagger that is intended to allow overlap of project schedules, yet minimize peak loading on all resources and the pressure to multi-task that is the usual result of these peak loads.

Effective multi-project management requires the stagger of projects in a way that does not put strain on the resources available to the organization yet maximizes organizational throughput.

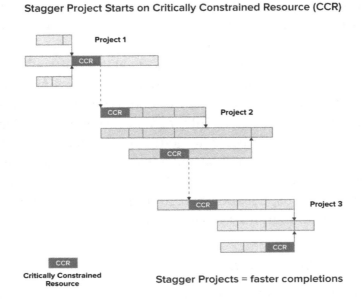

Stagger Project Starts on Critically Constrained Resource (CCR)

By having fewer active projects at any point in time, resources can address their focus to what is important to meet commitment in an effective manner. Fewer active projects result in a faster and more reliable stream of completed

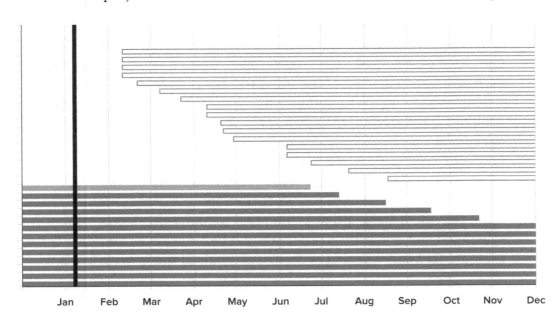

projects in this way. A faster stream of projects results in more projects completed in a given timeframe. So fewer projects result in more projects for the organization – more throughput – more profits, and at the same time provide more satisfaction and quality of work life for its employees.

The backlog of projects would look something like this:

Just as traffic engineers are focused on the flow of traffic by controlling the WIP, so should project-based organization focus on the flow of projects by controlling the WIP, and most certainty not on maximizing resource utilization.

What is the correct number of active/started projects?

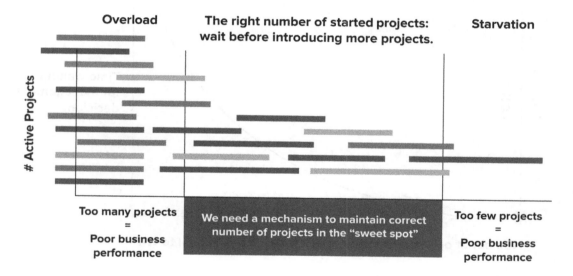

1. Release new projects at a pace that maintains the reduced load.
2. Do not release new projects too early; it will flood the system with work.
3. Do not release new projects too late; it will lead to starvation of work and unnecessarily extend projects' lead times.

Benefits

Pipelining projects reduces WIP:

■ This provides the potential for tremendous increases in productivity with minimal changes to operations.

- It's the most powerful and cost-effective tool for increasing production capacity.
- It's very simple to communicate and apply.
- It's great for fostering teamwork, as different areas become aware of the constraint and the need to work to assist the constraint.
- It provides immediate and very tangible benefits.
- It allows the growth of productivity without the need for additional staff.

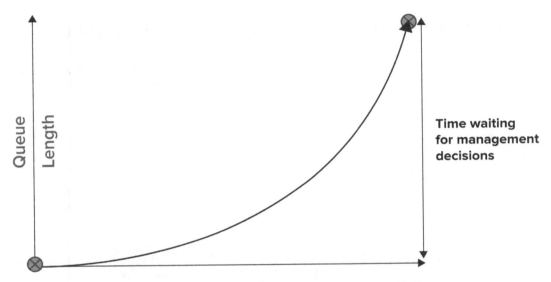

Number of open management decisions is proportional to WIP

Other benefits include the following:

Reduced resource contention. Pipeline sequencing of project starts eliminates much of the serious resource contention for the project team. Once the pacing resource (the drum) has been identified (or selected), resources are released into the pipeline

Reduced time waiting for decisions. With an increase in WIP, the number of decisions that need to be made by managers typically increases proportionately while a project is running. At a certain point, the wait time rises exponentially, as it does in any type of queue.

Modulating WIP ensures that decision time remains at an acceptable level, and does not impact the throughput of projects.

Increased throughput. By having fewer active projects at any point in time, resources can address their focus to what is important to meet commitment in an effective manner.

Fewer active projects result in a faster and more reliable stream of completed projects in this way. A faster stream of projects results in more projects completed in a given timeframe. So fewer projects result in more projects for the organization – more throughput – more profits, and at the same time provide more satisfaction and quality of work life for its employees.

Reduced multi-tasking. When you consider the duration-multiplying effect of multi-tasking, it should be clear that multi-project risks of cross-project interference could dwarf risks associated with individual projects. If project value is time sensitive, the delays suffered by projects due to resource time slicing across projects can be very expensive indeed.[6]

Reduced risk. The replacement of systemic pressure to multi-task with synchronization, combined with the management of resources for "relay race" behaviors, will go a long way to reduce risk and to speed project completions across the portfolio. In addition, the required careful consideration of the make-up of the pipeline and the active management of the critical resources identified and used as the synchronization mechanism will aid in understanding potential weak links for future improvement.[7]

Increase predictability. Senior management dislikes unpredictability. It makes everything more difficult, from planning cash flow to scheduling resources effectively.

There are many things that can be done to reduce unpredictability:

■ Reduce multi-tasking
■ Reduce WIP to increase flow
■ Underutilize non-constrained resources
■ Use early warning systems.

Simplifies task management. Improving your organization's flow is critical to creating an organization that can adapt to today's fast-paced world. Understanding what is limiting your ability to complete projects more quickly will allow you to provide clients and stakeholders with more accurate deadlines.

Better prioritization. Spending time optimizing non-constraints will not provide significant benefits; only improvements to the constraint will further the goal.

Summary

One of the key determinants of system throughput is the amount of work-in-progress (WIP). Too much WIP has a significant negative impact on throughput.

Starting a new project introduces more variables and therefore more complexity. If the system is unable to absorb this complexity, it will negatively impact the projects already in progress. Therefore, it's critical to determine what the system capacity is, and to ensure that the system is not over- (or under-) loaded.

This requires a way to stagger the introduction of new projects into the system instead of simply starting them as soon as possible. This is done by determining the critical constraint that limits the system's throughput. In projects, the main constraint is likely to be a specific resource pool (e.g. engineers, surgeons, etc.) that is shared among projects – the critically constrained resource (CCR). The capacity of the CCR determines when new projects can be started in order to maintain the flow of the system and not overload it.

Notes

1. Improving Focus, Predictability, and Team Morale on Projects. www.slideshare.net/JosephCooperPMP/pmi-congress-ccpm-final.
2. Program Management – TOC Multi-project Management. www.projectsmart.co.uk/white-papers/turning-many-projects-into-few-project-priorities-with-toc.pdf.
3. Program Management – TOC Multi-project Management. www.projectsmart.co.uk/white-papers/turning-many-projects-into-few-project-priorities-with-toc.pdf.
4. Thinking in Systems Flashcards | Quizlet. https://quizlet.com/50194660/thinking-in-systems-flash-cards/.
5. If You Are not Managing Your WIP, You Are not Managing. www.linkedin.com/pulse/you-managing-your-wip-company-jaco-laubscher.
6. About Contention for Other Resources Will Be with the Ability of Buffer. www.coursehero.com/file/p33rld4r/about-contention-for-other-resources-will-be-with-the-ability-of-buffer/.
7. About Contention for Other Resources Will Be with the Ability of Buffer. www.coursehero.com/file/p33rld4r/about-contention-for-other-resources-will-be-with-the-ability-of-buffer/.

Chapter 10

Resources

How Do You Schedule Resources in a Complex Environment that is Constantly Changing, and where Resource Requirements are Impossible to Effectively Determine Ahead of Time?

Ask yourself this question: Where do you get better service? At the store where all the assistants are busy, or the store where they are available to help you? At the restaurant where the wait staff have too many tables to serve, or where they have less tables to serve? At the call-center with the elevator music, or the call center with an open line? Which highway flows the best? The one where all the lanes are occupied or the one where there is excess capacity?

Obviously, the answer to all of these questions is the same: idle resources/protective capacity is required to provide good service. It's a no-brainer, yet for some reason project-based companies are still trying to keep everybody busy, all the time. Why?[1]

So why treat project resources differently? What makes you believe that pushing resource utilization to the maximum would yield larger profits for the company?

Common Practice

A goal of 100 percent utilization for all resources is an effective way to ensure the fastest project throughput.

The Problem

Organizations waste time trying to come up with plans that predict perfectly how much work a resource will expend on each task and then balancing the workload plans across projects. This does not work and will never work, since projects do not execute as planned.[2] It is futile to attempt to balance the workload for all project resources because tasks rarely land on someone's desk on a plan start date that was determined weeks or months in advance.

Many managers think that 100 percent utilization of people is a desirable state. But 100 percent utilization will kill your organization. Resource utilization on its own does nothing to increase project performance. Just because resources are busy is not necessarily a good thing.

If an organization activates projects just to keep the non-constrained team members busy, critically constrained resources quickly become over-allocated. In some project-based companies, high resource utilization is a key measurement, and the goal is to keep everybody, all the time. Projects are started just to make sure that there are enough active projects to book time against.

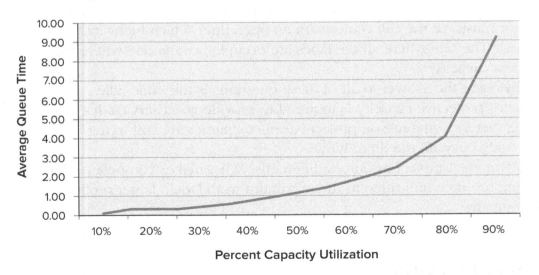

Average WIP Queue Increases Non–linearly with Capacity

Remember, if your staff is 100 percent utilized, 100 percent of your projects will be late.

Staggering projects based on the constraint resource automatically staggers projects for other resources, even overloaded ones.

■ By identifying the constraint, you've identified your true project capacity, making it easier to determine which and how many projects you can take on and the best sequencing of your projects.
■ Once the constrained resources are properly identified and managed, the scheduling of the projects typically allows the remaining resources to be scheduled as is convenient. When one looks at the new schedule of projects it becomes obvious that there is excess capacity in the non-constrained resources. This is not only OK; it is a necessary condition for success.
■ If one were to attempt to "balance" the organization by removing all the excess capacities, the entire set of resources will become constraints, and work will virtually come to a stop.

The Solution

To support the scheduling and monitoring of projects, however, the required process is far simpler than that usual approach: focus on maximizing flow through the system rather than trying to balance resource capacity.

Pipelining projects using the CCR maximizes throughput and greatly simplifies resource management.

Just as the critical path provides the focus for management regarding the most critical tasks, the CCR provides the management focus for resource scheduling and utilization.

Maximize the Constrained Resource

You don't want your constrained resource multi-tasking under any circumstances; instead, you make sure that projects organize their time around the availability of these resources.

When constrained resources are shared among projects, you can focus leveling on the constrained resource(s) and ignore the others. The resources that share their time between projects become the driving force for scheduling, budgeting, and creation of value. Others revolve around them.

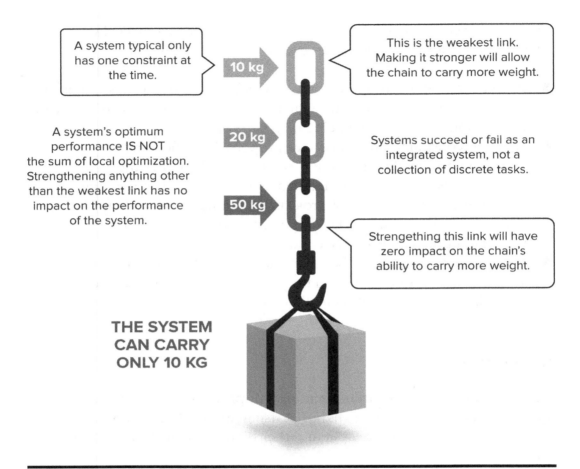

Figure 10.1   There may be many weak links but only one weakest link.

Ensuring that the CCR is fully utilized becomes a key management objective. It doesn't matter how effective your other resources are – the system will not increase production beyond what the CCR allows.

As posited by the Theory of Constraints:

So, when it comes to scheduling, effectively prioritizing tasks for the CCR is the primary goal of resource management.

Underutilize Non-constrained Resources

As WIP drops, the least constrained resources will start to run out of things to do. **This is a pivotal moment** – you have to avoid the temptation to either "load up" these resources with new tasks, or fire them as "excess capacity."

As unconstrained resources hold off on starting new projects, they will start sending less work to the constraint, causing throughput to go up. This is the lightbulb moment – when nearly everyone works less, and the company as a result produces more. It is not difficult at this point to convince everyone that their job is to do whatever it takes to maximize the constraint's productivity, instead of working as many hours as possible.

Tiago Forte, Praxis

By definition, any resource that is not critically constrained has additional capacity. This is necessary because you don't want the CCR to be delayed due to non-constrained resources not being available. By accepting that non-constrained resources will be underutilized, scheduling resources becomes much easier. Any temporary delay in the availability of non-constrained resources will be absorbed by the project buffer.

The scheduling of non-constrained resources therefore becomes less important because they are underutilized and therefore easier to make available as needed. This is a good example of sub-optimality in a CAS.

In fact, in order to maximize the CCR, it is *required* that other resources have sufficient protective capacity to protect throughput. If you were to attempt to "balance" the organization by removing all of the excess capacities, the entire set of resources will become constraints, and work will virtually come to a stop. Therefore the traditional goal of 100 percent utilization for all resources guarantees that all projects will be late.

Underutilized capacity

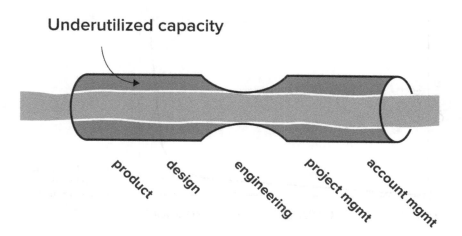

If one were to attempt to "balance" the organization by removing all the excess capacities, the entire set of resources will become constraints, and work will virtually come to a stop.

Therefore, it doesn't make sense to try to resolve each resource contention (bearing in mind that the actual time the work is performed is likely to be shifted due to the high variability) but rather for good enough smoothing of the load on each non-constrained resource pool. The temporary peak loads that remain in the plan are absorbed by the buffers. The level of "noise" of inherent variability in the projects would make such an exercise futile when it comes to project execution.

Once the constrained resources are properly identified and managed, the scheduling of the projects typically allows the remaining resources to be scheduled as is convenient. When one looks at the new schedule of projects it becomes obvious that there is excess capacity in the non-constrained resources. This is not only okay; it is a necessary condition for success.

Of course, if the critically constrained resources are optimally loaded, the non-constrained resources will be less than optimally loaded; even idle!

But as queueing theory shows, this is critical for faster throughput, because once you go above 80 percent utilization, queues grow exponentially.

Queuing theory *requires* that in order to achieve a systems maximum throughput, many parts of the system be idle at times.

The need for Protective Capacity

Growth in Queues vs. Growth in Utilization

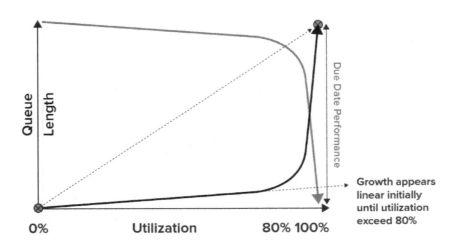

Removing "excess" capacity does two things:

■ it tells the employees that they must *never* be idle (and consequentially slow down the project stream);
■ it makes every resource a constraint.

The little savings realized by reducing excess capacities will inevitably be rewarded with a major reduction in the enterprise's overall capacity.

If the constaint is not overloaded — no other team can be overloaded

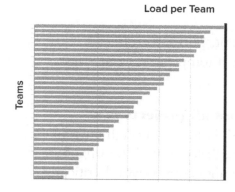

Load per Team

Solution:

• projects are paused until the constraints not overloaded any more

Result:

• perfect WIP
• all the other teams have protective capacity

Once the most constrained resource is no longer constrained, it is obvious that no other resource is constrained. (Wolfram Muller, Vistem)

This may feel inefficient to managers schooled in local optimization, but without subordinating the protective capacity, the smallest hiccup can cause them to become temporary roadblocks affecting the constraint and seizing up projects.

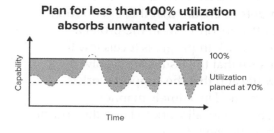

Plan for less than 100% utilization absorbs unwanted variation

100%
Utilization planed at 70%

Creates option to do the important things when you need it

Options

100%
Utilization planed at 70%

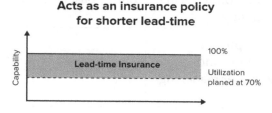

Acts as an insurance policy for shorter lead-time

Lead-time Insurance

100%
Utilization planed at 70%

Focus on System Capacity

Taking a higher level view of system capacity rather than resource capacity leads to the conclusion that it is enough to keep as little as one resource effectively utilized to manage and maximize the throughput of the system. Indeed, in order to do so, it is required that other resources have sufficient protective capacity to protect that throughput.

Therefore, determining a starting point for synchronizing the flow of work through the system can simply involve identifying an aspect of the multi-project system that can approximate its throughput potential.

Bear in mind that:

- Loss of output on the CCR has a permanent, pervasive effect.
- Loss of output on the other resources has a temporary, local effect.
- We need to protect the CCR.

Attempting to schedule all resources across all projects is a losing proposition. It has never proven possible to get enough current information together and processed quick enough to exceed the ongoing variations in all activities. Forecasting resource allocation beyond critically

Traditional Operating Assumption (The issue is not enough resources)	**Correct Operating Assumption** (Reducing the cycle time of projects will increase overall throughput)
Set aggressive resource utilization targets for the resource or skill even if cycle times increase. Keep work-in-progress levels high enough to ensure that resources do not run out of work. Subordinate all actions and decisions to keeping the resources busy. Focus improvement efforts on reducing the work content of each task.	Set aggressive cycle time reduction targets to ensure that there is no room for Parkinson's Law in the project. Keep work-in-progress levels low to ensure that the issues are resolved swiftly and that the support work is performed in a timely manner. Subordinate all work to keep the critical chain flowing (follow buffer-based-priorities).
Focus on reducing interruptions, streamlining issue-resolution and support functions, and better managing Parkinson's Law.	

constrained resources is impossible to predict because task deadlines are impossible to predict. There is also the variability of resource availability outside the control of the project manager, especially in multi-project environments with shared resources.

Focusing on reducing the cycle time of projects instead of increasing resource utilization is a major switch. Typically, organizations operate under the assumption that they are resource constrained. The table above contrasts the differences implied by focusing on cycle-time, not resources.

Is the Goal of the Organization Faster Throughput or Better Resource Utilization?

If your goal is to maximize the flow of work, you need idle resources ready and waiting. Maximizing flow and 100 percent resource utilization are in direct conflict.

- You can have a highway where the traffic flows, or you can have a highway where all the lanes are full of vehicles, but you cannot have both at the same time.
- You can have a restaurant with fast service, or you can have a restaurant where all the waitpersons are always busy, but you cannot have both at the same time.
- You can have busy people, or you can deliver projects quickly, but you cannot have both at the same time.

The little savings realized by reducing excess capacities will inevitably be rewarded with a major reduction in the enterprise's overall capacity.

Example

If electrical engineers were in very short supply and thus demanding a premium, a design organization might want to staff itself such that electrical engineers are its constraint. All other resources would have, on average, more design capacity so that the electrical engineers were always the bottleneck. Thus, management could plan the design workload such that electrical engineers were always at full capacity. As the electrical engineers completed tasks, they would "pull" more design work into the company.

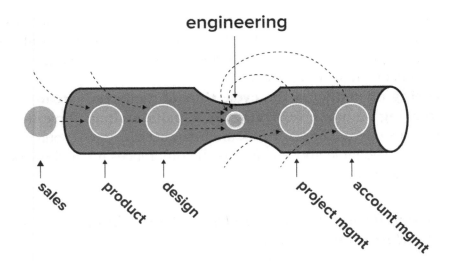

Pulling more design work into the company than the electrical engineers could handle would only serve to increase work-in-progress (WIP). This would slow down the organization and do nothing to increase its throughput. Electrical engineers would act as the "drumbeat" for the design organization much as a manufacturing bottleneck acts as the "drumbeat" for a plant.

The more work everyone sends to Engineering (which is the bottleneck in this system), the less time the engineers have to actually get things done. The less they produce, the newer projects everyone else starts "in the meantime", thus sending even more work to the bottleneck in a vicious cycle.[3]

Implement a Resource Wake-up Call System

Resource availability is monitored in anticipation of a new planned task. When a task on the critical path is about to be completed, the project manager (or the task manager) is prompted to check the current status of the resource needed for the next task and its level of readiness. The same applies to tasks on feeders. The objective is to ensure that the resource for the next task is aware of the updated situation with the current task and the anticipated time of starting the next task.

This procedure may be called "Resource wake-up call":

■ The system signals to the project leader/task manager, or to the project control room, that a resource will soon be needed for the next task.

- If necessary, actions have to be taken to guarantee their availability, especially for the tasks on the critical path.
- The wake-up call alerts the next resource on the critical path of the imminent date for the passing on of the task.
- The estimated completion date is updated every day based on the estimated completion date. The system calculates the time for the wake-up call by subtracting "the wake-up time" from the estimated completion date.

Summary

1. The focus is on the optimal utilization of scarcest resources. Critically constrained resources (CCR) typically represent less than 5 percent of the total number of resources – focus your attention here. They have that combination of skills and knowledge not found anywhere else.
2. Don't level all tasks for all resources. The level of "noise" or inherent variability makes trying to level all resources an exercise in futility when it comes to project execution.
3. Therefore, resource level the work of CCRs and let all the other resources around them be scheduled however they are by the team leaders.
   - All project managers use a single effective resource model to plan and execute their projects.
   - Resourcing, resource estimates, and resource utilization is consistent across all projects and used to allocate resources across all projects.
4. Don't assign a percentage of a resource. It makes resource management much more complex and encourages multi-tasking.
5. Assign and execute tasks according to the global priority.
6. Tasks on the critical chain are always done before non-critical chain tasks.
7. Within each group, tasks are executed by color (red/yellow/ green).
8. A new task is assigned to the first available resource (after finishing the previous task).

Since the CCR determines system throughput, the project/resource manager needs to focus on ensuring that the CCR is allocated to tasks as efficiently as possible. This is a lot easier than trying to schedule every resource involved in projects.

Notes

1. Still Pushing Resource Utilization? Don't You Know It. www.linkedin.com/pulse/seriously-you-still-pushing-resource-utilisation-dont-jaco-laubscher?articleId=6270905925389942784.
2. Chapter 9. Enterprise Resource Planning – Advanced Multi-project Management. www.oreilly.com/library/view/advanced-multi-project-management/9781604277340/9781604270808_ch_09.xhtml.
3. Theory of Constraints 104: Balance Flow, Not Capacity | Praxis. https://praxis.fortelabs.co/theory-of-constraints-104-balance-flow-not-capacity-60baa74ce9f4/.

Chapter 11

Monitoring

How Do You Determine the Status of a Project when Task Dates are no Longer Important?

You cannot understand a CAS by studying the individual parts. In Complex Adaptive Systems there is no simple method for understanding the whole by studying the parts, so searching for simple agent-level causes of system-level effects is useless.

If you run your project like a train schedule, a delay in a single segment on the journey is going to make the entire journey late. It therefore makes sense to focus on the individual segments and make sure they complete their part on time. It you remove a cog from a machine, the watch stops working.

But if a project is seen as a CAS, individual components of the system do not necessarily impact the overall system. If a duck falls out of a flock of ducks, the flock doesn't stop flying – the pattern changes but the flock continues on.

Therefore, monitoring a CAS requires a holistic view of the system. The focus is on the systems pattern of behavior rather than on the behavior of a single component.

For projects, the key is to focus on the project goal rather than on the individual tasks. Individual tasks can be late without having any impact on the project being completed on time.

Common Practice

The typical way to measure progress and provide current status goes something like this:

1. **Measuring project progress** against task deadlines gives a true picture of project status.
2. **Identifying risks** is a subjective exercise.
3. **Setting task priorities** is driven by task deadlines.
4. **Measuring task progress** by percent complete provides an accurate forecast of task completion.
5. **Evaluating team members** by their ability to hit deadlines ensures faster project completion.

The Problem

1. If **project progress** is measured against task deadlines, you have no protection against problems that will occur later in the project. In any event, given a relay race ethos implementation, task deadlines on the critical path are not tracked, and therefore cannot be used to monitor project progress.
2. There is no objective measure of **risk**, and therefore it is difficult to know when it is necessary to take management action and when it is not. In addition, there is no way to track the causes of risk, making ongoing improvement difficult to direct effectively.
3. **Task priorities** are driven by task deadlines without regard for the potential impact on the overall success of the project.
4. Percent complete is a poor measure of **task progress** – it tells you nothing about the future. It often paints an unrealistic or inaccurate

picture which can lead to a false sense of security. This false sense of security then leads to late-emerging issues which can cause re-scheduling of fundamental deadlines. Most importantly, it doesn't answer the main question: Are we on target?

5. **Measuring resource effectiveness** by the ability to meet deadlines is an easily gamed metric and encourages bad behavior, as described in Chapters 7 and 8 on estimates and scheduling. The solution to this problem is to use measurements that are tied to overall contribution to the success of a process or project.

The Solution

Monitoring and responding to the condition of the buffers is the key to project success.

Project Progress

In a complex world, conflicts are inevitable, making the ability to absorb shocks increasingly important. In engineering terms this is called resilience or the capacity to absorb energy elastically. The resilient model accepts that unpredicted threats will occur. Rather than establishing robust specialized defenses, a system that can encounter unforeseen events and can put the components back together and use the shocks to its benefit is required.

In project management, resilience is all about buffer management.

Monitoring and responding to the condition of the buffer is the key to project success. Buffer management for managing the project in execution provides a mechanism for measuring the acceptable consumption of the buffer and monitoring the potential impact it will have on meeting the required due date to the customer.

The project buffer is a safety instrument that is constantly monitored. It protects the project from disruptions that might happen when the activities on the critical path are performed. It protects the due date, is used to coordinate resources on the critical path (and have them ready when needed), and to prioritize work. Any task consuming the buffer is given the highest priority. Rather than responding to individual tasks, the project team responds to the condition of the buffers.[1]

The Buffer Burn Ratio

The buffer burn ratio (BBR) provides a running, leading status indicator. This indicator does not report the amount of work done. This is very different from most other project management methods, which tend to report project status in terms of work done ("We are 90 percent done!").[2]

The BBR is based on the ratio between the longest path through the project and the project buffer.

It represents work done in relation to how much time has been set aside (the buffer) to absorb unforeseen problems. It is a clear and unambiguous measure of project schedule status.

The extent to which this margin is consumed is an indication of the project's health or illness.

The BBR is like a feedback mechanism for a surfer, keeping them going while making adjustments as needed. It provides continuous process control and visibility even when the unexpected occurs, and facilitates rapid execution even if you have to take a detour.

- The BBR tells us the status of the project at any point in time – not only at a missed or hit milestone of due date.
- The BBR tells us when a project is in danger of not being completed on time.
- The BBR is a quick and effective measure for identifying work priorities, and can be used by management and staff at all levels without requiring sophisticated statistical analysis. By identifying which tasks are creating the highest buffer burn ratio, the project manager knows which tasks to focus on right now.
- Project execution decisions are based on buffer management. If a task takes longer than its aggressive planned duration, the buffer will shrink. If a task completes in less time than planned, the buffer will expand.

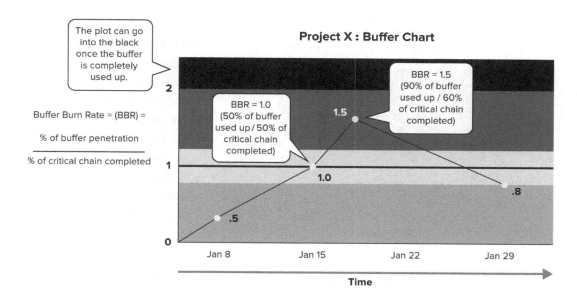

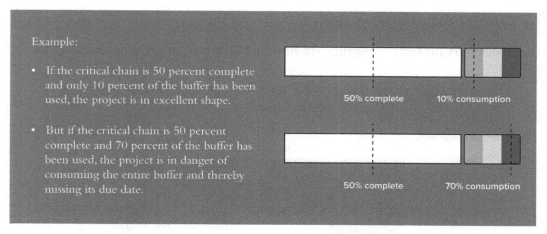

Project Status

The fever chart gives a visual signal without being concerned about the actual numeric value of the BBR.

The fever chart has a different purpose than the BBR: the borders between the red/amber/green (RAG) areas are inclined at different angles. The reason for this is that a fever chart typically has a different signaling logic.

The intent of a fever chart is to capture the "velocity" of buffer consumption (the BBR), and react early, as soon as it becomes unfavorable.

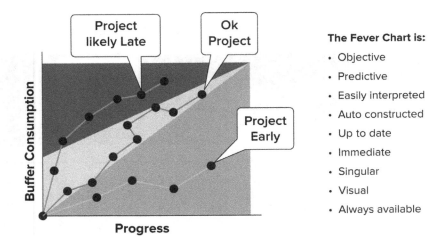

The Fever Chart is:

- Objective
- Predictive
- Easily interpreted
- Auto constructed
- Up to date
- Immediate
- Singular
- Visual
- Always available

The fever chart makes it very easy to see the status of a project at a glance.

The Buffer Fever Chart in Action

The fever chart provides a significant amount of information in a single chart.

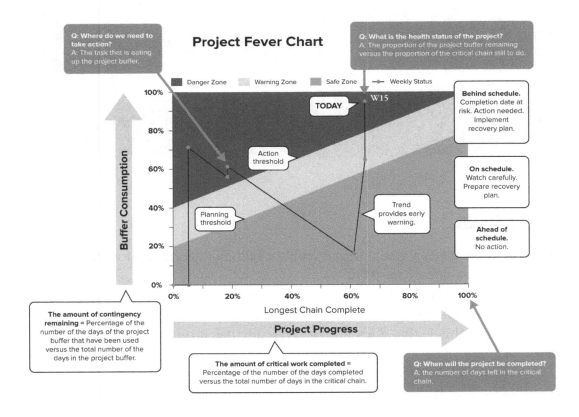

Include Feeder Paths on the Fever Chart

It is possible to show the buffer status of paths that are not on the critical path but merge with the critical path at some point. This is important because any delay in the feeder path would cause a delay in the critical path.

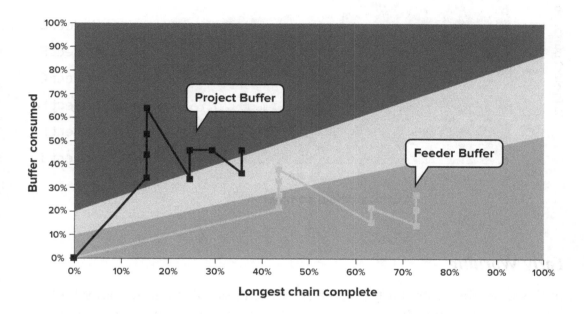

Show Multiple Project Statuses on a Single Fever Chart

Managing a portfolio of projects is not simply a question of managing the projects individually. They need to be managed so that each of them maximizes their contribution to the overall success of the company. Note that it is not about maximizing the result of every single project in isolation; it is about maximizing the result of the set of project outcomes as a whole for the company.

Therefore, it becomes very important to know how they are doing with respect to one another. It is beneficial to know what the buffer status is and how it is trending for all projects at the same time. How can this be achieved without information overload? It can be achieved very simply with a variation of the buffer fever chart.[3]

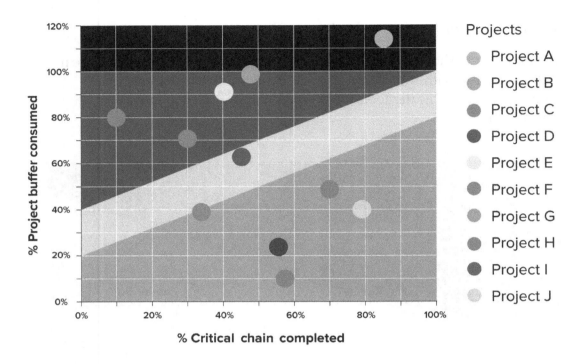

Early Warning

In this case, the fever chart gives earlier leading signals than the other buffer penetration diagrams, because it is based on buffer burn rate, not on buffer consumption. This way the fever chart will give you a very early leading signal. In practice, you should look for a "heads-up" on the fever chart

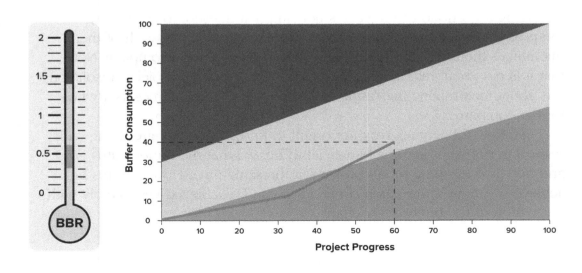

(buffer burn rate), and then for the confirmation on the other charts (buffer consumption). An integrated view shows the buffer consumption drawn as a thermometer on the Y axis of the fever chart: this gives you both signals in the same diagram.[4]

This is extremely powerful, especially because management can set the size of each zone based on past performance, inherent variability of the project, etc. Setting the size of each zone will in some regards define the degree of management involvement in the project.

Management should vary the percentages of buffer which fall into each segment using prior data from similar projects. If the project has a lot of uncertainty and as a result is deemed to be at a high risk of missing the schedule, management should drive the actions of the team by increasing the percentage of buffer which falls into the act or watch and plan segments. Defining the red, yellow, and green zones of projects' buffers is one of the high leverage controls which buffer management gives to project managers and senior management because the zones of the buffers can motivate the team's actions.

- The more time you have to respond to a delay, a problem, a change, a mistake, whatever, the more options you have, the more resources you can bring to bear on it, etc.
- When we have early warning about these things the chances of finding a solution or work-around are far greater. No one would dream of building a military base without a radar system to provide advance warning of a threat. It would be too vulnerable and it's unlikely it would survive. Running our mission critical projects without early-warning radar is just as dangerous. By the time we can see it, it's probably too late to do much about it.[5]
- It is not responding *after* the problem has done damage; it is to find the area of risk and respond *before* the damage occurs.

Risk Management

So what happens when trends penetrate through the various zones of the buffer?

Think of the fever chart as keeping the project within established control limits. This reduces the needless intervention changing of priorities and resource multi-tasking to a minimum.

During project execution, whenever an unacceptable buffer burn rate trend develops, the task or tasks causing the disturbance are quickly identified. Focusing the team on devising and implementing a specific recovery plan will keep the system in control.

This will transform project managers from being de facto task managers to try to truly manage the project. Obviously managing the performance of tasks is important. However, far more important is understanding which tasks are jeopardizing the delivery date while there is still enough time remaining for corrective action.

So, rather than responding to individual tasks, the project team responds to the condition of the buffer.

But it's important to recognize when to react to the buffer status.

What Happens when Trends Penetrate Through the Various Zones of the Buffer?

■ Whenever buffer penetration or trending thresholds are encountered, then is the time to act, before problems become critical. This is possibly due to the leading nature of these signals. These signals indicate that a risk is about to materialize; or, at least, the materialization's effects are about to impact the overall project schedule negatively.[6]

Common Cause and Special Cause

Buffer management clearly distinguishes between them and provides leading indicators that enable fast risk detection, categorization, and mitigation: the yellow zone is there to absorb common cause variation, while the red zone is there to absorb special cause variation.

It is critical to distinguish between two types of variance reasons:

■ A one-time occurrence of buffer penetration that is likely due to a **special cause,** i.e. a one-time exceptional circumstance;
■ A recurring reason that indicates a systematic problem due to a **common cause**. Common cause variation is inherent in the process itself, and provides the opportunity to initiate process improvement.

**One of the most devastating errors in risk management is to
confute the two kinds of risks.**

Statistical Process Control Chart
(How a project behaves over time)

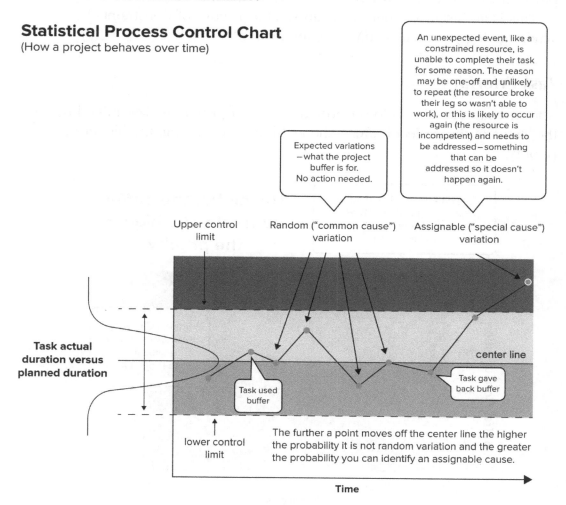

An unexpected event, like a constrained resource, is unable to complete their task for some reason. The reason may be one-off and unlikely to repeat (the resource broke their leg so wasn't able to work), or this is likely to occur again (the resource is incompetent) and needs to be addressed – something that can be addressed so it doesn't happen again.

Expected variations – what the project buffer is for. No action needed.

Upper control limit

Random ("common cause") variation

Assignable ("special cause") variation

Task actual duration versus planned duration

center line

Task used buffer

Task gave back buffer

lower control limit

The further a point moves off the center line the higher the probability it is not random variation and the greater the probability you can identify an assignable cause.

Time

Trigger Conditions and Reason Codes

By deliberately finding a reason, you are actually identifying a risk that is
about to become a problem. Any time you discover a new reason, you have
uncovered a new unmanaged risk. Whenever you decide to take action,
annotate the corresponding reason code, document the trigger condition,
and the action taken (preventive, mitigation, avoidance, etc.). This provides
a systematic way to identify where we can improve the process in a more
focused way than typical "process improvement" initiatives, like CMMI and
similar ones, where all and everything is "improved" all the time.[7]

Not everything is worth improving; only the most common or expensive problems. Focus efforts where they can have the most effect.

This is an instance where you can see the Theory of Constraints in action, giving you focus and leveraging power.[8]

Task Priorities

A fever chart can also help set priorities. Project priority is determined by the status of the project buffer – the less buffer remaining, the higher the priority.

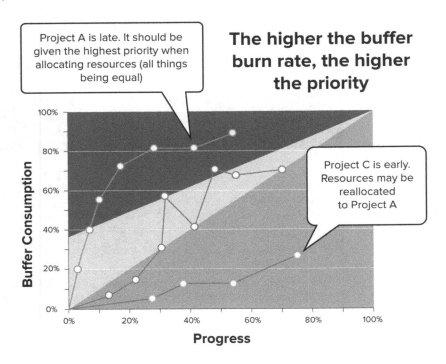

Of course, this requires management judgment: just because Project A is in the red zone, and Project C is in the green zone doesn't necessarily make Project A more important.

The key question is: **What are the implications if Project A or Project C is late?**

The trend chart helps managers understand the likelihood of different projects being late.

By making the actual priorities of all tasks transparent to everyone in the organization, buffer management ensures that task owners know what to work on, and that managers know which tasks to focus on or shift resources to help.

Appropriate Priority Setting

Instead of tasks being prioritized using arbitrary means – like whichever manager cries the loudest for their task to get done – is one. Or it might be as simple as which task a person prefers to work on, or which task arrived to me first, etc. By making the actual priorities of all tasks transparent to everyone in the organization, you ensure that task owners know what to work on, and that managers know which tasks to focus on or shift resources to help. So it's not magic when critical path reports that more projects get done on time.[9]

This makes priorities transparent so that we can always focus on the right things.

Task Progress

The Problem with Percent Complete

Percent complete is a poor measure of progress

Percent complete:

- cannot be challenged – only the task owner knows;
- is often simply aligned with time used;
- doesn't tell when a task will be completed;
- leads to persisting "90 percent complete";
- is not an objective metric, so can cause major/incorrect re-scheduling.

When looking at the percent complete of multiple tasks, percentage complete for each task in terms of the project status becomes meaningless.

What is the Status of This Project?

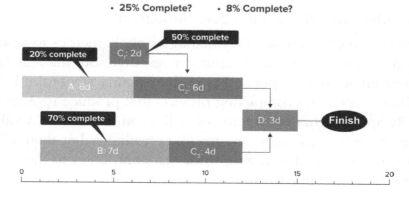

Percent complete has no relevance to the future

Asking a task owner about percent complete simply focuses their mind on the past and it is impossible to change what has already happened.

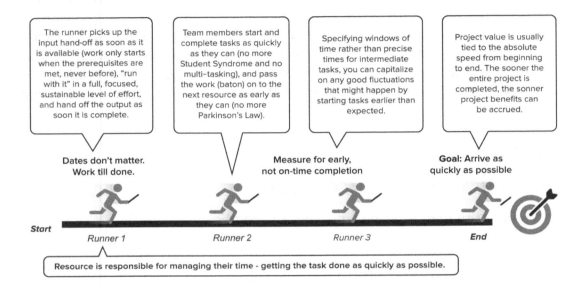

Progress measurement by deadlines obscures the relative priority of work

Just because a deadline for a task is looming doesn't automatically make it the highest priority. Using deadlines to determine priority often results in time and attention being spent on non-essential, non-value-added activities.

Everything is equal, including critical tasks and non-critical tasks, so focus is diffused and obscured.

Resource utilization doesn't measure throughput

In an effort to control costs, many managers apply metrics to resource utilization – a measure of raw output per resource. But the real value is not in individual "output" per se but in the resource's contribution to the overarching objective – completing projects that produce revenues and profits. By applying the cost metric of utilization rather than a value metric that assesses outcomes, managers may be creating rather than solving problems. Instead of encouraging work that contributes to the business, they are rewarding busy work.[10]

Extrinsic rewards destroy intrinsic motivation

Setting explicit outcome-based targets with associated incentives destroys intrinsic motivation (i.e. people start chasing the target without considering potential consequences). Another way to put it:

Other Problems with Measurement and Metrics

Progress measurement by deadline encourages the wrong behavior.

People are accountable for meeting their individual deadlines instead of being accountable for their overall contribution to the success of the project. It makes people defensive, forcing them to defend their original delivery promises, and giving "reasons" for why things haven't quite worked out.

To be effective, measurements should:

■ induce the parts to do what is good for the whole;
■ direct managers to those parts that need their attention.

What We Really Need to Know?

What do we really need to know?

The only meaningful measurement of project status is the answer to this question:

When will the project be complete?

To answer this effectively, we need to know:

• How exposed are we?
• Have we got enough safety in hand?
• Is there a trend? Is it upward or downward?
• Should we be taking any action?
• Where should we be taking action?

Instead of asking for the percent complete for a task, the question to ask is:

When Will This Task be Completed?

This will provide the remaining duration for the task. This is the only data element you need to collect.

Asking for remaining duration is a much harder question to answer than percent complete. It requires consideration of all sorts of issues. Managed properly, the estimate to complete (remaining duration) becomes a fresh commitment from the task owner to the project as a whole to achieve a specific, short-term, and measurable result. It prompts asking: What can we do to help?

Status Reporting on the Critical Path

Users have their own visualization of how much buffer their task is consuming:

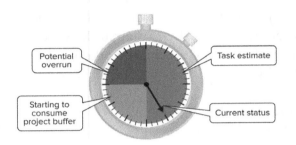

Task Consumption Dashboard

Users have their own visualization of how much buffer their task is consuming.

If users are given a visualization of the status of their tasks on an ongoing basis, they will be more inclined to try to stay within the challenge time, and if that's not possible, to ask for the necessary help.

If users are given a visualization of the status of their tasks on an ongoing basis, they will be more inclined to try to stay within the challenge time, and, if that's not possible, to ask for the necessary help.

The key to effective buffer management is frequent status collection. The remaining duration may be a different number every day. The task being worked on depends on the difficulties and successes that have been achieved that day as well as the best estimate of how many days remain from right now. The remaining duration may therefore be a different number every day.

Since this approach is so simple, it can be updated daily without wasting anyone's time. The quicker managers are aware of potential problems, the faster they can shift priorities to accommodate and get the schedule back on track.

This is an example of a high leverage point in the information structure of the system. It's not a parameter adjustment, nor a strengthening or weakening of an existing feedback loop. It's a new loop, delivering feedback to a place where it wasn't going before. This simple difference resulted in significant benefit – a perfect example of CAS non-linearity.

Status reporting is integral to the final project deadline: expected start and end dates are automatically recalculated by the system based on estimated completion date. The calculation would take into account any kind of relative scheduling (e.g. Task B must start before Task F can begin).

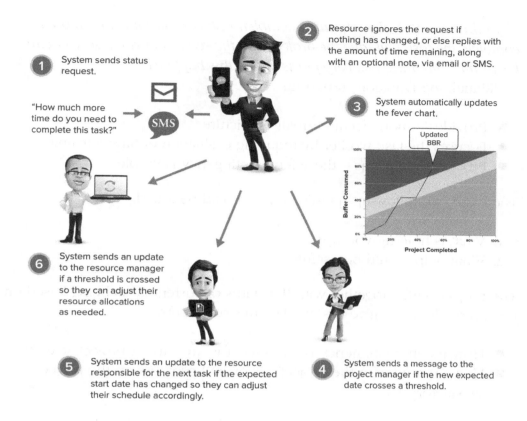

Management Early Warning

The buffer chart is updated automatically as the status is reported, and the manager is alerted automatically if there is a boundary cross-over in the fever chart. This provides an early warning if there is going to be a potential consumption of buffer.

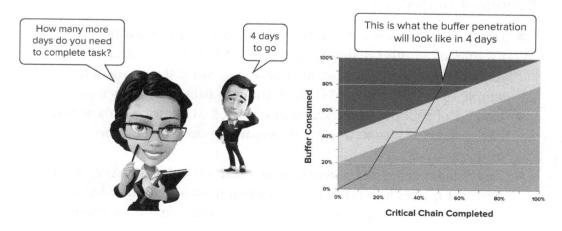

In this example, the estimated completion based on four days more to complete the task will take the project into the red buffer area, so you can begin implementing recovery plans before this happens.

"Remaining Duration" reporting:

- Provides a more accurate/realistic picture.
- Focuses the task worker by requiring evaluation of time remaining.
- Provides real status – the safety contingency is visible.

There are two follow-up questions that should be asked:

1. What is holding you up?
2. What help would be useful?

The project buffer, together with the status of current tasks being based on remaining duration, gives us two key measurements:

- How much contingency is left? (What is my current project status?)
- How far are we in the project? (Is overall progress on the project satisfactory?)

The key is to track the only most meaningful measure of project status: When will the project actually be complete? Managed properly, the estimate to complete (remaining duration) becomes a fresh commitment from the task owner to the project as a whole to achieve a specific, short-term, and measurable result. It prompts asking: *What can we do to help?*

Reporting Frequency

- How often status is communicated is a critical prerequisite for effective buffer management. A key to effective buffer management is frequent status collection. Since this approach is so simple, it can be updated daily without wasting anyone's time.
- Instead of reporting task status in terms of work done on a weekly basis, status is reported as work remaining on a much more frequent basis.
- Daily status helps keep people's attention on one task. Asking the person for remaining duration has them thinking about what they still have to do. It also becomes a subtle commitment for them.

- If you get a frequent status update from everyone working on tasks, you have a much better chance of catching problems early, especially if you use buffer penetration as your metric.
- This also gives the next person a more accurate heads-up when things will be coming.
- As tasks are completed, we know how much they have eaten into or replenished the buffers. Because we are now getting updated estimates of time-to-completion from currently active tasks, we can stay on top of how much of the buffers are consumed in an ongoing fashion. As long as there is some predetermined proportion of the buffer remaining, all is well.[11]
- If task variation consumes a buffer by a certain amount, we raise a flag to determine what we might need to do to if the situation continues to deteriorate. If it deteriorates past another point in the buffer, we put those plans into effect.
- This process allows us to stay out of the way of the project resources if things are on track, build a contingency plan in something other than a crisis atmosphere, and implement that plan (disrupting everyone's life) only if necessary.

Example

1. Resource A needs Resource B to do something to help them complete their critical task.
2. Resource B cannot start the task for another four days.
3. If the four additional days are still within challenge time for the task, nothing needs to be done.
4. If not, by reporting that the task will be completed four days later than the expected time (i.e. it needs to consume some project buffer), the appropriate managers are alerted and they can try to negotiate more time.

Step Consumption Dashboard

The step consumption dashboard provides a view of how much buffer steps in a process are consuming project buffer. If a step contains sub-processes, the step will show the highest consumption rate in the hierarchy, and the user can drill down to see the steps on each level.

1. What tasks are on the critical path.
2. Project status (percent critical path outstanding).
3. Project buffer status (red, amber, green) (action required?).
4. Feeding buffers status (red, amber, green) (action required?).
5. Tasks in progress (to ensure earliest completion in full).
6. Tasks not started. to ensure earliest start where appropriate).
   - ■ Effective due-date protection and extra effective capacity
   - ■ More reliable on time in full to budget delivery performance.
7. Identification of critical path and feeding chains focus.
8. Buffer flexibility and a stable plan.

	Completed	The step has been successfully completed
	Active	Started, not consuming buffer
	Monitor	Has started to consume buffer
	Act	Consuming significant buffer
	Late	Beyond estimated duration
	Waiting	Task or sub-process should have started but is delayed
	Skipped	Step has been skipped

					Steps							
Project	1	2	3	4	5	6	7	8	9	10	11	12
P123												
P124												
P125												
P126												
P127												

Measuring People Performance

One of the key changes is how people are measured and managed.

- ■ Individuals are not penalized or in any way measured by task deadlines. Dates can be set as a guideline, but that's all it is. It is not a commitment, and therefore does not have consequences.
- ■ Since uncertainty in projects exists, and fluctuations during task execution depend on the severity of obstacles encountered, among other things.
- ■ So, there is no direct way of measuring if a person is under-performing or is faced with uncertainties. Also, through imposing aggressive task duration times, it is expected that not all tasks are performed within the planned estimates of the durations that were made.
- ■ Therefore, resources are not asked to report their work progress in percent of completion, since this assumes fixed task durations and focuses on the amount of work done. In the monitoring and

control process, the constant question is the amount of work that is left to do for each task.

■ Since task deadlines are not a true measure of performance, it cannot be used for reporting status. Individual task completion dates and milestones are de-emphasized to avoid sub-optimization. Rather, the team is evaluated as a unit on overall project completion.

■ Measure based on work packets (typically processes) – reward the team based on their success in meeting the target without going over the buffer. Everyone in the work packet is focused on the buffer consumption. *All* team members involved in that work packet are notified when a buffer boundary has been crossed.

■ At any given moment, everyone can see the task causing penetration of the critical path and thus know the effect that early or late delivery is having on the project. Crucially, because the information is logically derived from objective data, everyone knows it is valid, and can thus trust the need to subordinate their own actions to what is best for the whole. Everyone knows where to pay attention – and you can take timely, unified, course-correcting action.

Benefits

Status Reporting is Simplified

The system prompts the participants for the number of days remaining on their current task(s) on a daily basis. They can ignore this prompt if the number of days remaining hasn't changed. The system automatically updates the buffers and schedule with any changes, and warns the manager if a boundary has been crossed in the fever chart.

This:

■ Eliminates the need for participants to remember to report status.
■ Keeps status up to date on a daily basis.
■ Eliminates the need for project managers to ask for status or have status meetings.
■ Eliminates the need for managers to get involved unless tasks start consuming significant buffer.

With this kind of visual reporting, status meetings, review meetings, etc. can be focused on the troubled spots. The approach will also give ideas about where help can come from and prevents team territoriality from developing. The common agreement is about everybody collaborating and collectively taking the best actions that benefit the organization as a whole, rather than just a single team or project.[12]

Buffer Management Provides Early Warning

Too often project management artifacts are backward-looking and record historic or past effort. They do not provide the visibility to effectively manage current and remaining task durations or resource contention. This results in switching task priorities, instability, and ever-increasing chaos.

When we have early warning about these things the chances of finding a solution or work-around are far greater. No one would dream of building a military base without a radar system to provide advance warning of a threat. It would be too vulnerable and it's unlikely it would survive. Running our mission-critical projects without early-warning radar is just as dangerous. By the time we can see it, it's probably too late to do much about it.[13]

> It is not responding *after* the problem has done damage; it is to find the area of risk and respond *before* the damage occurs.

Buffer management provides the necessary forward-looking information to overcome emerging sources of delays with greater flexibility, resulting in keeping projects on schedule, within budget, and delivered on time. Just as importantly, buffer management alerts you to when no additional extraordinary actions are required if the project is within the previously established control limits.

Project Buffers Encourage Teamwork

- When the team shares an aggregated buffer and is primarily judged on overall project success, it promotes offloading non-essential tasks from constrained resources.
- A shared buffer encourages team members to pass on early finishes so that the team can increase project buffer.
- Shared buffers promote constructive peer pressure. When a team shares an aggregated buffer, they are much more dependent on

each other for success and will "push back" against teammates who unnecessarily waste the buffer. When resources have their own safety time, they feel that it is theirs to use, even if it is not needed. When the safety time is community property, the dynamic is completely different.

Buffer Management Facilitates Optimization

Tracking reasons for substantial buffer consumption facilitates ongoing improvement by eliminating the causes of delay.

Buffer Management Measures are Fact-based and Objective

- Remaining duration, rather than typical status monitoring which provides a rear-view look into the project rather than a forward-looking one, gives a more realistic picture of a project's progress, and focuses the task worker by requiring evaluation of time remaining.
- Buffers can be used to manage a project through simple numerical measurements, which can be compared across projects. Buffers also provide a simple means for communication both within and between projects. This can provide a global metric and help managers to apply their limited resources to the tasks that will have the greatest impact on the money-making ability of the company.
- It takes very little energy to understand what's relevant because BBR boils down the current status of a project to a highly visual one page of information. Time doesn't need to be spent bringing people up to speed, or gathering status updates.
- This allows meetings to be not only shorter, but to more effectively engage the team in an analysis and communication of the job flow status and diagnosis of issues, such as bottlenecks, unresolved problems, etc.
- The team then collaborates on the actions needed to take corrective action, such as resource assignments during the day, issue follow-up, etc.
- Analysis of buffer consumption allows project managers to focus their energies on the highest leverage tasks. This allows critical management time to be used more efficiently and helps avoid

demoralizing micro-management. Management is encouraged not to micro-manage by the "green" buffer management area and to manage only high leverage tasks.

Buffer Management Enables the Project Manager

Buffer management frees up management time to manage only the few important things that are momentarily causing significant buffer impact, rather than the much larger quantity of items for which no management involvement is required. It also provides focus for schedule management, avoids unnecessary distraction, and allows recovery planning to take place when needed, but well before the project is in trouble. Armed with advanced knowledge of schedule risk, managers can proactively adjust priorities and resource assignments to ensure timely project delivery.

Buffers provide a project manager with the following:

■ A simple, objective measure of project progress relative to the committed project date – at any time.
■ A simple, objective measure of project health.
■ A simple rule for triggering – and not triggering – corrective action.
■ The ability to prioritize tasks objectively – both within and across projects.
■ Automated status collection.

Always visible safety contingency:

■ Elimination of persisting "'90 percent complete" syndrome.
■ Less likelihood of late-emerging issues.
■ Provides a combined view of progress *and* contingency.
■ Trends provide early warning.

Summary

Looking at individual elements of a CAS tells you nothing about the state of the whole. Neither does the focus on a particular point in time because the environment is constantly changing. You need a holistic metric that is able to discern patterns over time and provide an early warning that things may be headed in the wrong direction.

Because buffers have been aggregated, it is assumed that the percentage of buffer consumed at any point in time should be less than or equal to the percentage of the critical path being completed. If the buffer is being consumed faster than the project is progressing, it is possible that the project may not complete in time.

By focusing on buffer consumption, you get a holistic, objective measure of how well the project is doing, allowing you to act before it becomes too late. This is much more effective than the typical use of "task percent complete" as a measure of project status.

Notes

1. Buffer Management and Risk Management in the Theory of. … https://chronologist.com/blog/2012-10-04/buffer-management-and-risk-management-in-TOC/.
2. Buffer Management and Risk Management in the Theory of. … https://chronologist.com/blog/2012-10-04/buffer-management-and-risk-management-in-TOC/.
3. Visual Portfolio Management – The TameFlow Chronologist. https://chronologist.com/blog/2014-11-25/visual-portfolio-management/.
4. How to Draw Buffer Fever Charts – The TameFlow Chronologist. https://chronologist.com/blog/2017-03-30/how-to-draw-buffer-fever-charts/.
5. Why Critical Chain "Works" – Viable Vision. www.myviablevision.com/critical-chain-works/.
6. Buffer Management and Risk Management in the Theory of. … https://chronologist.com/blog/2012-10-04/buffer-management-and-risk-management-in-TOC/.
7. Buffer Management and Risk Management in the Theory of. … https://chronologist.com/blog/2012-10-04/buffer-management-and-risk-management-in-TOC/.

8. Buffer Management and Risk Management in the Theory of. … https://chronologist.com/blog/2012-10-04/buffer-management-and-risk-management-in-TOC/.

9. Why Critical Chain "Works" – Viable Vision. www.myviablevision. com/critical-chain-works/.

10. Blindsided! – pinnacle-strategies.com. http://pinnacle-strategies.com/wp-content/uploads/2018/11/blindsided-five-invisible-project-threats_v09.pdf.

11. Because We Are Now Getting Updated Estimates of Time to Completion From. www.coursehero.com/file/p6flv0q5/Because-we-are-now-getting-updated-estimates-of-time-to-completion-from/.

12. Visual Portfolio Management – The TameFlow Chronologist. https://chronologist.com/blog/2014-11-25/visual-portfolio-management/.

13. Why Critical Chain "Works" – Viable Vision. www.myviablevision. com/critical-chain-works/.

Chapter 12

Optimization

How Do You Optimize a Complex Environment?

Because a CAS is non-linear, optimizing a CAS means finding leverage points within the CAS that can provide non-linear returns (i.e. where small changes can provide significant results). The obvious focus should be on leveraging the current system constraint. Leveraging the constraint means doing everything possible to ensure that the constraint is as efficient as possible. Then look for the next constraint and repeat.

A second way to optimize is to take advantage of the lowly checklist as a simple way to implement attractors and boundaries. Checklists can act as soft boundaries and attractors to help ensure that agents in the system (project participants) are always aware of the guidelines they need to apply in any situation so as not to exacerbate the complexity of the environment. Checklists are an excellent way to eliminate easily avoidable errors and omissions, and to "nudge" people in the direction you want them to go without having to create and enforce rules.

Lastly, we see multi-tasking as a way to get multiple things done faster. This is of course a myth, and has the impact of creating more complexity through uncertainty and unpredictability. Reducing multi-tasking where it counts is another simple way to decrease the amount of complexity in your environment.

Leverage Constraints

TOC seeks to provide a precise and sustained focus on improving the current constraint until it no longer limits throughput, at which point the focus moves to the next constraint. The underlying power of TOC flows from its ability to generate a tremendously strong focus toward a single goal and to removing the principal impediment (the constraint) to achieving more of that goal.[1]

By doing so, you are releasing management from the natural tendency to try to address everything (in effect, focus on nothing), resulting in a failure to improve. Managing a complex system can be made simpler and more effective by providing managers with a few specific focus areas on which to focus – maximizing performance in the areas of key constraints.[2]

A constraint is a positive, not a negative. It is an opportunity for management to focus on what matters, instead of wasting their time focusing on everything.

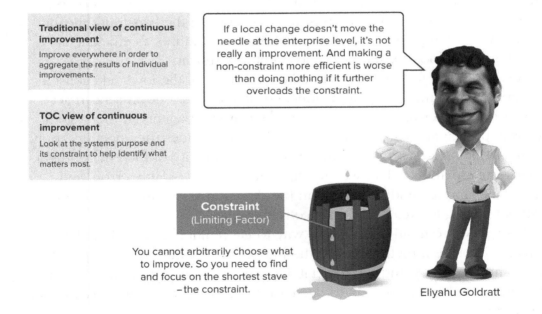

Traditional view of continuous improvement

Improve everywhere in order to aggregate the results of individual improvements.

TOC view of continuous improvement

Look at the systems purpose and its constraint to help identify what matters most.

If a local change doesn't move the needle at the enterprise level, it's not really an improvement. And making a non-constraint more efficient is worse than doing nothing if it further overloads the constraint.

Constraint
(Limiting Factor)

You cannot arbitrarily choose what to improve. So you need to find and focus on the shortest stave – the constraint.

Eliyahu Goldratt

A Process of Ongoing Improvement

"Put Everybody to Work"

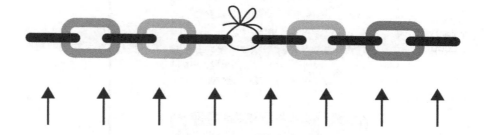

Process Improvement Teams

Limited time, energy and resources are spread
across the whole system, instead of being focused
on the one part of the system that has the potential
to produce immediate system improvement:
the constraint. People soon get
discouraged when they see no tangible system
resulting from the dedicated effort they have put
into process improvement.

TOC is based on the idea that in any complex system at any point in
time there is only one, or at most very few, aspects of the system keeping
that system from achieving more of its goal (and what are problems but
impediments blocking you from reaching a goal?). These constraints, if
properly identified and broken, provide the fastest route to significant
improvement for the system and can provide the basis for long-term,
strategic improvement.

Focusing Steps

Five focusing steps are at the heart of TOC and the various applications are
derived from them.

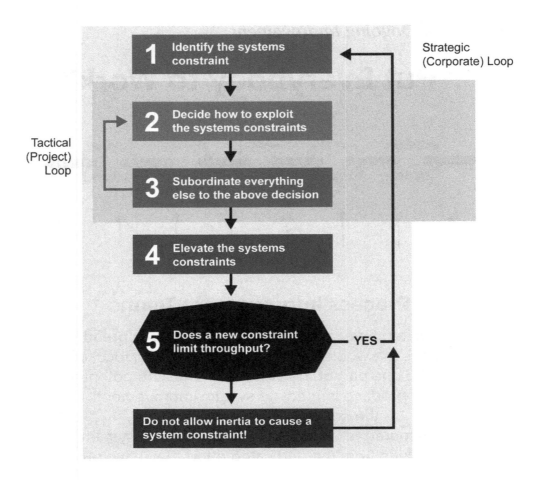

Step 1: Identify the Constraint

Finding the constraint is covered in Chapter 9 on execution.

Step 2: Maximize the Constraint

How should we manage the constraints, the things that we do not have enough of? At least, let's not waste them. Let's squeeze the maximum out of them. For example, if the constraint is a specific internal resource, it means ensuring that it is productive all of the time.

To maximize the constraint, make certain:

■ it is doing what it should be doing; it stops doing what it should not be doing;

■ it is not being wasted by, for example, doing things that can be done by someone else, or doing more than is needed;

■ it has the right amount of work to be effective;

■ it has what is needed to do the job (may include skills/ information/data/knowledge, or reliability of partners/vendors);

■ it is protected from delays in other parts of the system (remove limitations that constrain the flow, and reduce non-productive time, so that the constraint is used in the most effective way possible);

■ there aren't rules or business practices that inhibit the maximization of the constraint;

■ non-constraints are not in the way of the constraint.

Step 3: Subordinate Everything Else (to Maximizing the Constraint)

What is subordination?

Subordination means, for example: making sure that the constraint is not waiting for work; helping the constraint to work faster by offloading unnecessary work; and linking the output of other operations to suit the constraint;

How easy is it to subordinate?

This is the most important and the most difficult of the five focusing steps to accomplish. Why is it so difficult? Because:

1. It requires everyone and every part of the system not directly involved with the constraint to subordinate, or "put in second place", their own cherished success measures, efficiencies, and egos.

2. It requires everyone, starting from top management going down to all levels, to accept the idea that excess capacity in the system at most locations is not just acceptable – it's actually a good and necessary thing![3]

3. Subordination formally relegates all parts of the system that are not constraints to the role of supporters of the constraint. This can create behavioral problems at almost all levels of the company.

4. It is very difficult for most people to accept that they and their part of the organization aren't just as critical to the success of the system as any other. Consequently, most people at non-constraints

will resist doing the things necessary to subordinate the rest of the system to the constraint.

What does subordination practically mean?

- Subordination simply means that every decision made and every action taken by the entire organization must be done based on its impact on the constraining resource.
- Units of work should be pre-prepared and pre-packaged to make sure that the constraint never has to wait around for additional data, content, information, or decisions.
- There should be a buffer of work ahead of the constraint so that the constraint never runs out of work and goes idle. This means that the person or team before the constraint must have excess capacity, to be able to build up a buffer (or queue) of work-in-progress. It also makes sense for the upstream resources to spend time carefully packaging this work for easy "consumption" by the constraint.[4]

Step 4: Elevate the Constraint

When the second and third steps are complete and we still have a constraint, then is the time to move to the fourth step.

The next step is intuitively obvious. If we do not have enough, it does not mean that we cannot add to it. For instance, when the constraint has been a machine in the plant, this is the step in which you will add physical capacity.

(Note: This is the fourth step, not the second step.)

Elevate means to "Increase Capacity", "Lift Restrictions". If the constraint is an internal resource, this means obtaining more time for that resource to do productive work.

Some typical alternatives for doing this might be to acquire more machines or people, or to add overtime or shifts until all 24 hours of the day are used.

If the constraint is market demand (i.e. lack of sales), elevation might mean investing in advertising or new product introduction to boost sales.

Increase the capacity of the constraint by:

- Overtime or hiring more staff.
- Reducing setup time for the constraint (full kitting).
- Investing in process improvements for the constraint.

- Buying more capacity.
- Moving work away from the constraint (work done by others, subordination, outsource).
- Re-sequencing for improved processing.
- Checking quality *before* the constraint (prerequisites).
- Improving quality after the constraint (post-requisites).
- Any other action that removes the constraint.

Step 5: Go back to Step 1 (Do Not Let Inertia Set In)

By the fourth step, we have helped the company move forward. Can we stop here or must we add a fifth step?

The answer is once again intuitively obvious. If we elevate the constraint, if we add more and more to the things that we didn't have enough of, there must come a time when we do have enough.

The constraint is broken. The performance of the company will rise, but will it jump to infinity? Obviously not. The performance of the entire company will be restricted by something else. The constraint has moved.

So, if, in the previous step, a constraint has been broken, go back to step 1. Do not let inertia to set in!

Integrate Checklists

Checklists are typically given little respect in most organizations. Yet checklists are a powerful way of providing attractors and boundaries in a CAS like project management.

In a CAS, there are many ways to get things done, and the way you choose should depend on the current context. Checklists provide a balance between the imperative to do something in a particular way with the freedom to make adjustments to meet the needs of the circumstances at hand.

When checklists become part of a unit of work:

- The checklist is immediately made available to the user when they are notified to start a step. There is no need to have to look for it or remember to use it.
- Checklists can automatically lock that step so that the process cannot continue until the checklist has been completed.

- This provides an audit trail which ensures that users have completed what they are supposed to do.
- Checklists help shorten work transitions by assuring the next person in the process that the previous step has been fully completed and does not require any follow-up to make sure things have been done.
- Checklists can spawn additional tasks to do the work required by the checklists item, thereby keeping everything in context.
- Checklists can be updated on the fly, so the checklists are always up to date.

Types of Checklists

Routine checklist. With a routine checklist, you write down all the steps/tasks needed to complete a certain project or process. The list of tasks never changes. You use the same checklist over and over again every time you do that particular process/project.[5]

Success checklist. This type of checklist describes the normal successful actions.

Failure checklist. This type of checklist illuminates the negative scenarios we can anticipate.

Learning checklist. When an incident or problem or change review captures that an error was made, we fix the checklist. And when a situation was created that we had never foreseen, we create a checklist for how to deal with it next time.

Awareness checklist. This type of checklist is designed to make the person more aware of the current situation and act accordingly. For example, "Please note the weather conditions. Based on these conditions, should the anti-ice be on or off?" or "How is the patient's skin color different from yesterday?" If you ask questions that encourage mindfulness, you bring people into the present and you're more likely to avoid bad results.[6]

How to Make an Effective Checklist[7]

Simply making a list of the steps involved in a certain task does not an effective checklist make. Here are some tips from *The Checklist Manifesto* to help you create a truly useful checklist:

- Investigate your failures and look for "killer items".
- Examine why you aren't getting the results you want.
- Look for failure or friction points in the tasks you do routinely. These failure or friction points will serve as the basis for your checklist.
- You don't need a checklist that lists every single step on how to complete a task. That renders a checklist useless. Instead, just focus on putting down the "stupid" but essential stuff that you frequently miss.
- Decide if you need a "communication" checklist. Most checklists are likely procedural (they lay out things you need to do), but some tasks or projects are so complex that communicating with others becomes vital to managing all the moving pieces. In such a case, create a dedicated communication checklist and make sure it includes who needs to talk to whom, by when, and about what.

The Benefits of Checklists[8]

A checklist might be the best way to model complex, unstructured, ad hoc processes. When a process is not predictable, putting a lot of work into an elaborate diagram is not worthwhile.

Users can create dynamic checklists based on what has occurred previously. Issues that have come up repeatedly with a step can be noted, along with a sub-checklist of what the user must do if such an issue arises.

Checklists verify that the necessary minimum gets done. With increasing complexity comes the temptation to skip over the stupid simple stuff and instead focus on the "sexy" parts of one's work. Because the stupid simple stuff is so stupid and simple, we often fool ourselves that it's not important in the grand scheme of things. But it's often our most basic tasks that can spell the difference between success and disaster. Checklists remind us to make sure that the stupid, simple, but absolutely necessary stuff gets done.

Checklists free up think time. Offloading the need to remember basic tasks frees up the brain to concentrate on the important stuff. For surgeons, this means that they're left with more time to focus on handling unforeseen problems that often come up when you're slicing someone open.

Checklists instill discipline. Because checklists provide a binary yes/no answer, they instill discipline in the person who uses it. Research shows that giving someone a checklist for a task increases their chances of completing it. There's something about having a checklist that spurs people to get stuff done. Perhaps it's the dopamine rush that comes with checking something off, or the concreteness which checklists provide, or a combination of the two.

Checklists save time. A common complaint about checklists is that they take too much time to go through. But running through a checklist need not take very long, and research shows that doing so will actually save you time in the long run. Because checklists can prevent errors caused by skipping basic steps, you spend less time fixing mistakes and more time doing constructive work.

Checklists provide an audit trail. By forcing the person responsible for completing a task to actively check off the items in the checklist, they are in effect confirming that they have indeed completed these steps. If a problem occurs later that is a result of missing one of the checklist items, management can go back to the person responsible to find out if they really did complete the checklist item. If they did not, they should not have checked off the item as complete.

Checklists allow you to you push the power of decision making out to the periphery and away from the center. You give people the room to adapt, based on their experience and expertise, constrained by checklist items that must always be done regardless of the decisions made.

Eliminate Bad Multi-tasking

Obviously, the more things you have going on at any one time increases the uncertainty and unpredictability of your environment (and therefore the complexity) and quite likely the environment of others who depend on the output of your work.

Good Multi-tasking vs. Bad Multi-tasking

Bad multi-tasking is when someone is waiting for the output of your task before they can do their work. So not all multi-tasking is bad. When nobody is waiting for your output there is nothing wrong with switching between various tasks. It may not be efficient, but it may not matter.

This section is focused on reducing the impact of bad multi-tasking.

Multi-tasking multiplies the time to complete a task

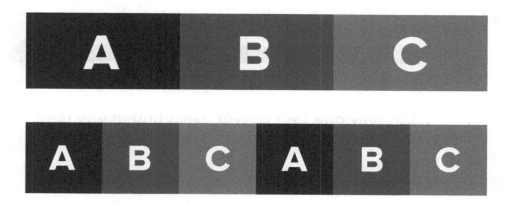

A and B are delayed, with no gain for C...
...no one wins.

Allowing team members to focus on their tasks sequentially rather than multi-tasking is, counter-intuitively, a very effective solution to most organizations' need to do more with less.[9]

As is illustrated below, significant improvements can be made by allowing team members to focus on their tasks until completed. When organizations begin to realize the significant productivity improvements that can be gained by simply reducing multi-tasking, a new level of organizational performance can be achieved, creating a decisive competitive edge over the competition.

The Problem

When someone stops doing a task on the critical path and starts doing something else, they are delaying the entire project.

The reason for this should be quite intuitive. If you interrupt work on one project prior to handing it off to work on another project, one project sits idle while work is performed on the other. This results in longer lead times for all the individual projects involved.

Whenever I put down one task and pick up another, I lose productive time:

All available tasks appear to be executing...

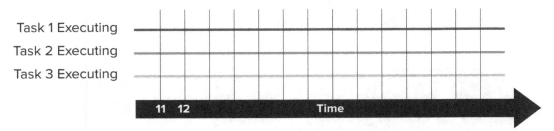

...but only one task is ever executing at any time.

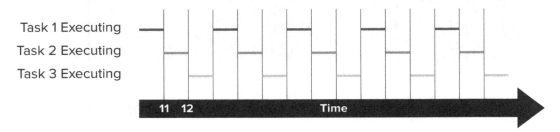

If a resource divides its attention between different tasks before handing off task deliverables, all the projects involved will take longer than necessary because all of that resource's successors on each project will have to wait longer than necessary due to time spent on other projects' work.

And if many resources in the organization become accustomed to working in this manner, then most projects will take significantly longer than necessary in both their promise and their execution.

The projects will also be impacted by the variability of not only their own tasks but also of those associated with the other projects that are interleaved within them.

One of the key challenges of multi-project or program management therefore revolves around the avoidance of pressures on resources to multi-task and the ability to assess and direct the most beneficial use of resources when there is apparent contention for their attention. To the extent that these can be addressed, a multi-project program will minimize the pain encountered in the interaction of projects fighting for shared resources.

Multi-tasking:

- Slows everything down;
- Complicates scheduling and control;
- Reduces quality;
- Removes planning predictability;
- Wastes time and costs more;
- Causes delivery delays;
- Is bad for morale.

The Solution

Eliminating (or at least reducing) multi-tasking results in a significant improvement in the ability to predict the duration of a specific task. There are many ways in which multi-tasking can be reduced, including adopting a relay race ethos, and most importantly by reducing WIP.

People can easily be involved with more than one project without multi-tasking as long as they complete the individual tasks they are involved in before moving to the other project's task. If, however, they bounce back and forth, both projects suffer due to the time spent on the other one.

- When someone starts a task, they stick to it until it's completed.
- Each task starts only when the right resource is available and the prerequisite tasks are complete.
- Each task is completed as quickly as possible.

The Problem

One resource
3 x 1 day tasks
All needed
"today"

Day 1

Solution #1 — Multi-task

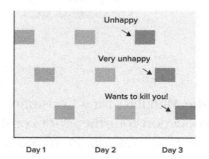

Unhappy

Very unhappy

Wants to kill you!

Day 1   Day 2   Day 3

Solution #2 — Don't Multi-task

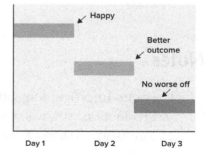

Happy

Better
outcome

No worse off

Day 1   Day 2   Day 3

Benefits

Allowing team members to focus on their tasks sequentially rather than multi-tasking is, counter-intuitively, a very effective solution to most organizations' need to do more with less. When organizations begin to realize the significant productivity improvements that can be gained by simply reducing multi-tasking, a new level of organizational performance can be achieved.[10]

Single-tasking:

- Improves quality;
- Enables planning predictability;
- Reduces time and money spent;
- Is good for morale;
- Simplifies scheduling and control;
- Speeds everything up.

In addition, cash flow improves when you don't multi-task:

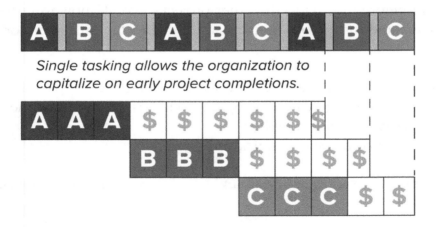

Single tasking allows the organization to capitalize on early project completions.

Notes

1. Focus Improvement on the Manufacturing Constraint | Lean Production. www.leanproduction.com/theory-of-constraints.html.
2. Ray Ison, *Systems Practice: How to Act in Situations of Uncertainty and Complexity in a Climate-change World.*
3. Constraint Management – SlideShare. www.slideshare.net/utkanuluay/constraint-management-40285197.

4. Theory of Constraints 108: Optimizing the Constraint. https://medium.com/praxis-blog/theory-of-constraints-108-optimizing-the-constraint-512162cd6548.

5. How and Why to Use Checklists | The Art of Manliness. www.artofmanliness.com/articles/the-power-of-checklists/.

6. Mindfulness in the Age of Complexity – hbr.org. https://hbr.org/2014/03/mindfulness-in-the-age-of-complexity.

7. How and Why to Use Checklists | The Art of Manliness. www.artofmanliness.com/articles/the-power-of-checklists/.

8. How and Why to Use Checklists | The Art of Manliness. www.artofmanliness.com/articles/the-power-of-checklists/.

9. Improving Focus, Predictability, and Team Morale on Projects. www.slideshare.net/JosephCooperPMP/pmi-congress-ccpm-final.

10. Improving Focus, Predictability, and Team Morale on Projects. www.slideshare.net/JosephCooperPMP/pmi-congress-ccpm-final.

Chapter 13

Implementation

People don't resist change. They resist being changed.
Peter Senge, The Fifth Discipline

Many of the ideas presented in this book would seem to require changes in human behavior – things like procrastination, multi-tasking, unnecessary polishing of already finished work, etc.

But the behaviors that support conventional project management are deeply embedded as a result of decades of past experience and training, formal processes, and performance measures. To make a quantum leap difference to the success rate of your projects, these behaviors need to change.

But trying to change behavior directly usually meets with strong resistance, and changing behaviors in a large organization can take forever. Yes, you might get some initial successes by focusing on behaviors, but they won't last.

Complexity Science suggests that we can create small, non-threatening changes that attract people, instead of implementing large-scale change that excites resistance.

So, the answer is to "nudge" employees to adopt new behavior by implementing new policies, systems, and measurements in ways that don't change them.

Nudging

> We empower everyone to nudge their systems in a direction
> appropriate to their context … start doing small things in the
> present, rather than promising massive things in the future,
> because that just leaves perpetual disappointment.
>
> *Dave Snowden*

Nudge is a concept in behavioral science, political theory, and economics
which proposes positive reinforcement and indirect suggestions to try to
achieve non-forced compliance to influence the motives, incentives, and
decision making of groups and individuals.[1]

Nudges are small changes in the environment that are easy and
inexpensive to implement.

With a nudge, we could get people to do whatever is best for them
without prohibiting anything or imposing fines, or restricting their behaviors
in any other hard way.

A nudge makes it more likely that an individual will make a particular
choice, or behave in a particular way, by altering the environment so that
automatic cognitive processes are triggered to favor the desired outcome.
However, this can have the opposite outcome, so care must be taken as
to what behaviors are being rewarded in effect rather than in theory. For
example, imagine measuring a doctor's performance based on how many
people they treat. It incentivizes the doctor to "treat" and count the numbers
treated rather than maintain good health and well-being in the community
(which of course reduces the number of people being treated).

Examples of Positive Nudging in a Project Management Environment

Some of the most helpful "nudges" to be found in a project management
environment include the following:

- Instead of insisting that individual tasks finish on time, use measures that
  drive low work-in-progress. You'll reduce multi-tasking and increase on-
  time delivery.
- Create enough buffer (typically 50 percent of total task time) to
  ensure that work flows without interruption. Placing buffer time

where paths intersect keeps people from waiting for hand-offs, and allows work to progress unimpeded.

■ Whereas individual tasks may be late, make the project due date sacrosanct. Analyzing the reasons behind buffer consumption will help managers respond to the root causes of delays and keep the overall project on schedule.

Others include:

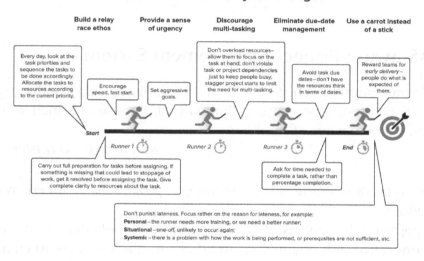

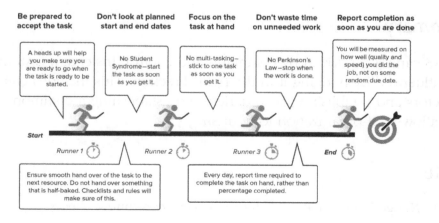

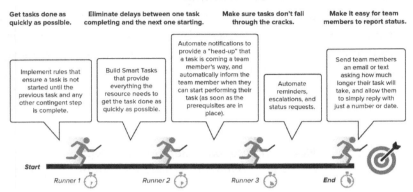

How to nudge team members to adopt the desired behavior: System

A CAS-aware Project Management System

> If you want to teach people a way of thinking, don't bother trying to teach them. Instead, give them a tool, the use of which will lead to new ways of thinking.
>
> *Richard Buckminster Fuller*

Another type of nudging is implementing a project management system that users adopt.

By applying the lessons of CAS, we can build tools that are more robust, more innovative, self-organizing, and that can quickly adapt to changes in the environment.

This is by far the simplest and fastest way to implement the ideas in this book.

Summary

A CAS cannot be driven by command and control. Instead, a CAS must be influenced by nudging it in the right direction. This includes creating attractors and establishing boundaries, and establishing a common vision that allows self-organization to flourish.

Note

1. Nudge Theory | Psynso. https://psynso.com/nudge-theory/.

Chapter 14

Benefits

Shifting Paradigms

The difference is subtle, but it completely changes how you manage your projects.

Old Paradigm	New Paradigm
Tasks must be padded to handle uncertainty.	Remove padding from tasks. Create a project-level buffer to handle uncertainty.
If task deadlines are met, the project will come in on time.	Don't use task deadline dates. Only the project date counts.
Using the critical path is the way to determine the project timeline.	Don't use the critical path alone. Constrained resource management is as equally important as the critical path.
Multi-tasking allows resources to get many tasks done faster.	Eliminate multi-tasking on critical tasks. Single tasking allows users to get tasks done faster.
Overlapping project starts gets more projects completed faster.	Delay project starts until the system can absorb them. Staggered project starts get more projects completed faster.
Task percent complete and task deadline tracking is the best way to measure project status and performance.	Stop using percent complete to determine task status. Use buffer management to measure project status and performance.

continued

Continued

Old Paradigm	New Paradigm
Keep everyone busy – assign as many tasks to each resource as needed to keep them 100 percent busy.	Don't worry about keeping everyone busy.

Benefits Overview

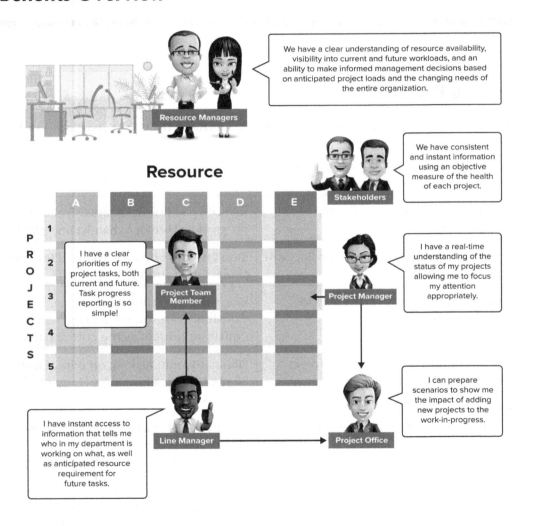

Project Team Member Benefits

Simplified Project Management	Simplified Project Measurement
■ Clearer priorities ■ Resources get to work as soon as possible and work as quickly as possible ■ No need to multitask – expected to deliver one thing at a time ■ No reason to make the work fill a specified amount of time ■ Go as quickly as possible on each leg they own ■ Pass it to another team member as quickly as possible	■ Less stress ■ Reduced fear of failure – no due dates ■ Much simpler progress reporting – dedicated to a single task and periodically report how many days are remaining ■ No multi-tasking and fewer interruptions ■ More motivation ■ The Relay Runner Work Ethic motivates effective performance to get the project done on time

Project Manager Benefits

Simplified Project Management	Simplified Project Measurement
■ Clear focus for project manager (critical chain, reduced early start) ■ Simplified project status reporting ■ Significantly reduced need for schedule changes and priorities ■ Whether to plan or act decided by measurement ■ Resource priorities decided by measurement ■ Focusing on buffers eliminates unnecessary distractions ■ Buffers provide early warnings, facilitates recovery planning when needed, but well before the project is in trouble ■ Less, and more focused, status meetings with the shift of focus away from "what we've done" via reporting percent of work complete to focusing on what counts to assess and address project status – how much time is left to accomplish unfinished tasks	■ Quick and easy plan status ■ Real-time project status – no need to wait for reports ■ Immediate focus by buffer, chain, and task provided by status ■ Decisions defined by buffer report ■ Focus of buffer reporting on management priority decisions (reflected in the buffers by staggering project start) ■ Unambiguous, objective progress measurement leaves no room for interpretation ■ Persisting 90 percent complete syndrome is eliminated by focusing on expected completion date ■ Simpler ongoing improvement, determining areas that need improvement through the analysis of buffer/contingency consumption rates and tasks with excessive variability

Organizational Benefits

Less	More
<ul><li>Stress for employees, managers, and leadership overtime</li><li>Demand on management attention</li><li>Incentive to hide problems and look for scapegoats, since 50 percent of tasks are expected to be late</li><li>Waste when multi-tasking</li><li>Need to hide actual completion time</li><li>Need to constantly change the schedule through the elimination of task deadline scheduling</li><li>Room for interpretation, blaming, and complaining by providing unambiguous, objective progress measurement</li><li>Rear-view mirror watching by focusing on buffer penetration, not on past performance</li></ul>	<ul><li>Job satisfaction, motivation, and morale</li><li>Types of behaviors needed for effective teams</li><li>Forward-looking perspective through predictive/preventative/leading reporting</li><li>Encouragement and promotion of teamwork</li><li>Ability to resolve project issues before they impact due date</li><li>Holistic/goal-oriented perspective</li><li>Neutral, normalized performance measuring metrics</li><li>Clear communications between team members, project managers, with each other, and project managers with management</li><li>Sense of urgency by removing task padding and using a relay race approach</li><li>Empowerment to help team members finish work as early as possible</li><li>Clear accountability</li></ul>

Traditional vs. CAS-aware Project Management Methods[1]

Traditional Project Management	CAS-aware Project Management	Expected Benefits
Schedule is based on worst-case task durations (90 percent chance of success).	Schedule is based on average task durations (50 percent chance of success).	■ Padding is removed from individual tasks – now everyone shares the risks equally among all tasks and resources. ■ Safety time is conserved and used most wisely over the entire project. Focus is placed on what is most important to the customer: speedy deliverables.
Emphasizes task progress.	Emphasizes project progress.	■ Everybody sees the "Big Picture". ■ Micro-management is avoided. ■ Project managers have a consistent outlook throughout the entire project. ■ Events that slow the project are constantly in the schedule spotlight. ■ People stay focused on the problems. ■ Problems get identified more quickly, and ■ get solved sooner.
Starts tasks that are not on the critical chain ASAP.	Starts tasks that are not on the critical chain only when they need to be started (so they don't impact the critical chain).	■ Constrained resources are impacted by non-critical tasks which block and slow critical tasks. This is similar to fire lanes and sirens on emergency vehicles. ■ Non-critical traffc stays off the roads until the emergency vehicles have passed. ■ Use of bottleneck resources is based on priority, not "first come, first served". Projects get completed faster.

continued

Continued

Traditional Project Management	CAS-aware Project Management	Expected Benefits
Starts and finishes all tasks at scheduled start and finish times.	Starts critical chain tasks as soon as predecessors are done, finishes tasks as quickly as possible.	■ The project is managed and implemented like a relay race. The baton always goes around the track at maximum speed. Runners pace themselves for hand-offs so that the baton never stops or slows down. If you are carrying the baton, just finished carrying, or getting ready to carry it next, your activities are tightly monitored, controlled, and managed; all others are of lesser priority and have freedom to self-manage. ■ People focus better, and projects get done faster and more cheaply.
Makes resource contention a "fact of life".	Resolves resource contentions explicitly.	■ Constrained resources are identified by the schedule. All users of the critical resource are identified up front and conflicts resolved. ■ Project managers watch only the critical resource; constantly focusing on what's important and preventing problems from occurring. ■ Constraints are managed.
Makes multi-tasking a "fact of life".	Minimizes multi-tasking by setting priorities.	■ The cost of multi-tasking is exposed. ■ People hunt down and eliminate their own multi-tasking, multi-tasking forced on them by others, and multi-tasking done by others.

continued

Continued

Traditional Project Management	CAS-aware Project Management	Expected Benefits
Reacts to uncertainty by changing priorities, expediting, and creating a new schedule.	Manages uncertainty by monitoring impact of events on buffer consumption.	■ The impact of one project on all other projects is minimized. ■ Entire organization stabilizes into busy and productive status quo activities, rather than chaos. ■ People are more productive, less frustrated, involved. Their contributions and efforts matter. Morale climbs.
Makes task linkages and constraints reflect ad hoc or habitual scheduling decisions.	Makes task linkages and constraints reflect only physical scheduling requirements.	"Sacred cows" like "we've always done it that way" get challenged.

Note

1. Adapted from Differences between Critical Chain (CCPM) and Traditional. http://pqa.net/ProdServices/ccpm/W05002003.html.

Conclusion

> Managers, I think, should now get ready to face the full complexity of their organizations and economic environments and, if not control them, learn how to intervene with deliberate, positive effect. Embracing complexity will not make their jobs easier, but it is a recognition of reality, and an idea whose time has come.
>
> *Richard Straub, Managing Uncertainty, Harvard Business Review*

Despite the potential for significantly better outcomes, CAS approaches to project management can be visibly uncomfortable for managers who need to feel in control of a documented project plan, and to organizations that look to traditional practices and certified practitioners to feel more confident in their investments.

Unfortunately, complexity isn't a convenient reality given managers' desire for control. The promise of applying Complexity Science to business has undoubtedly been held up by managers' reluctance to see the world as it is. Where complexity exists, managers have always created models and mechanisms that wish it away. It is much easier to make decisions with fewer variables and a straightforward understanding of cause and effect.[1]

In project management, it's much easier to spend time creating and maintaining a detailed schedule than it is to spend time helping make sure that things are done as quickly as possible. We know task deadlines are always going to change – and yet we persist in creating artificial deadlines.

With the right attitude and the right software, implementing this new approach is relatively painless when compared to the enormous benefits that can be expected. The key is accepting complexity and the impact of complexity in managing projects.

It's an opportunity to gain a competitive advantage with very little investment. Why not give it a try?

Note

1. Why Managers Haven't Embraced Complexity – hbr.org. https://hbr.org/2013/05/why-managers-havent-embraced-c.

Bibliography

Advanced Multi-project Management – Achieving Outstanding Speed and Results with Predictability, Gerald Kendall and Kathleen Austin, November 1, 2012, J. Ross Publishing.

A Leader's Framework for Decision Making, Dave Snowden and Mary Boone, November 2007, *Harvard Business Review.*

Be Fast Or Be Gone, *Racing the Clock with Critical Chain Project Management*, Andreas Scherer, March 18, 2011, ProChain Press.

Complexity – A Guided Tour, Melanie Mitchell, April 1, 2009, Oxford University Press.

Critical Chain Project Management, Third Edition, Lawrence P. Leach, July 11, 2014, Artech House.

Critical Chain, Eliyahu M. Goldratt, April 1, 1997.

Embracing Complexity: Strategic Perspectives for an Age of Turbulence, Jean G. Boulton, Peter M. Allen, and Cliff Bowman, July 30, 2015, Oxford University Press.

Lean Project Leadership, Lawrence P. Leach and Shane P Leach, January 4, 2010, BookSurge Publishing.

Project Management in the Fast Lane – Applying the Theory of Constraints, Robert C. Newbold, March 25, 1998, CRC Press.

Projects and Complexity, Francesco Varanini and Walter Ginevri, May 9, 2012, Auerbach Publications.

Projects in Less Time – A Synopsis of Critical Chain, Mark J. Woeppel, December 1, 2005, Pinnacle Strategies.

Reaching the Goal – How Managers Improve a Services Business Using Goldratt's Theory of Constraints, John Arthur Ricketts, October 23, 2007, IBM Press.

Smart Process Apps – The Next Breakout Business Advantage, Jonathan Sapir and Peter Fingar, November 20, 2013, Meghan-Kiffer Press.

Systems Thinking Made Simple – New Hope for Solving Wicked Problems, Second Edition, Derek Cabrera and Laura Cabrera, August 6, 2018, Plectica LLC.

Systems Thinking – Managing Chaos and Complexity – A Platform for Designing Business Architecture, Third Edition, Jamshid Gharajedaghi, August 9, 2011, Morgan Kaufmann.

The Billion Dollar Solution – Secrets of Prochain Project Management, Robert C Newbold, November 27, 2011, ProChain Solutions, Inc.

The Goal – A Process of Ongoing Improvement, Eliyahu M. Goldratt, July 1, 2014, North River Press.

The Critical Chain Implementation Handbook – Flow Is The Number One Consideration, David Updegrove, June 5, 2014.

The CIO's Guide to Breakthrough Project Portfolio Performance – Applying the Best of Critical Chain, Agile, and Lean, Michael Hannan, Wolfram Muller, and Hilbert Robinson, August 7, 2014, Fortezza Consulting, LLC.

Theory of Constraints, Eliyahu M. Goldratt, January 1, 1990, North River Press.

Theory of Constraints Handbook, James F. Cox III and John G. Schleier, Jr., May 6, 2010, McGraw-Hill Education.

Thinking in Systems – A Primer, Donella H. Meadows, February 5, 2009, Chelsea Green Publishing.

Visual Project Management: Simplifying Project Execution to Deliver on Time and on Budget, Mark J. Woeppel, December 1, 2005, Pinnacle Strategies.

Index

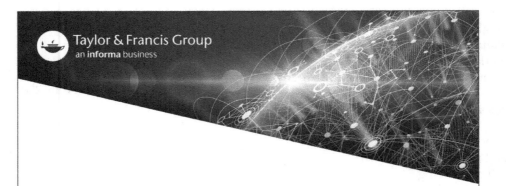